WHICH
ONE IS
YOU?

Done with life's bullshit. We all need to live, next!

ALYSSA FRANK

authorHOUSE®

AuthorHouse™ UK
1663 Liberty Drive
Bloomington, IN 47403 USA
www.authorhouse.co.uk
Phone: UK TFN: 0800 0148641 (Toll Free inside the UK)
*   UK Local: 02036 956322 (+44 20 3695 6322 from outside the UK)*

Published by AuthorHouse 09/17/2020

ISBN: 978-1-6655-8009-0 (sc)
ISBN: 978-1-6655-8010-6 (hc)
ISBN: 978-1-6655-8011-3 (e)

Contents

Chapter 1

PUSSY-WHIPPED

P ussy-whipped means that a woman is holding a man's cojones (balls), and he allows it.

We've all experienced it firsthand or we know someone who has; we pitied them, made fun of them, dated them. And one ultimate question pops into our minds every time we are at the mall and see a tiny little fellow, with a despaired look in his face, while his woman paints his fingernails with different nail polishes, to see which one she likes: *What's wrong with you, dude?*

"Pussy-whipped" may sound offensive, derogatory, and even insolent. But for better or worse, it brilliantly encapsulates the behavior displayed by men when they are utterly controlled by their stronger romantic partner. The pants are worn by the woman; the sturdy-willed counterpart dictates the what, the where, the how much, and the when of the relationship. What's in it for the guy, anyway? Getting laid (perhaps).

But unfortunately for these fellows, being dominated in this sense has nothing to do with the image of Christian Grey and his six-pack blindfolding you and whispering naughty things in your ear. Nope, better picture Niles Crane from *Frasier* to get a better idea. His wife never even appeared in the show, yet everyone knew he was enslaved, influenced, pussy-whipped (see, the term is excellent).

In fairness, most men need to be tamed a bit in order to be in a serious relationship. Giving up their bachelor way of living is somewhat expected once they take a girlfriend or wife. And aside from a drunken cousin, no one makes fun of them. "Hey Johnny, you drove your wife to the hospital to give birth and canceled bowling night with the guys? You are so pussy-whipped," said … no one ever. Except for drunken cousin Bill.

The problem is, like many things in this glorious life, when that delicate balance between what's normal and expected, and what's crazy and creepy gets altered. In other words, when women walk over their men, and they permit it. These women control every aspect of their life (even when the woman is asleep, busy, in another country, or under surgery, they want to know everything).

There is no better way to understand this ordinary, bizarre, and disturbing behavior than with signs. Signs are useful; they lead you to discover what you have ignored and acknowledge what you have been reluctant to accept. So without any other distractions, here's the ultimate list of signs you are a pussy-whipped:

1. Permission granted or not: You need her permission. "For what?" you may ask. I would say, "For whatever." That single phrase is just not right. You are dating or are married to someone; you're supposed to share essential responsibilities like paying rent and deciding who turns the bedroom light at night. (I told you we should've gotten a night lamp for each one of us!) You are not supposed to have a boss, but a partner. When going for a beer requires permission, sometimes in writing (true, sad story), you are submitting yourself to your power-hungry partner. She foresees that going to a pub may mean trouble for her; you know, mingling with other joyful human beings to celebrate life for a while is heavily frowned upon in her twisted set of values. It may begin innocently, like when you asked her permission to change your date night because you had a work trip; but suddenly, you find yourself friendless and begging your woman if you can skip keto diet on Monday night because all the housecleaning (yes, dear, I did not forget the curtains and rags this time) left you exhausted, and you're dying for some pasta.

2. Decision-making: She makes the decisions. Entirely related to the above sign. Not only do you need her continuous permission; she has managed to grant herself a seat at the Decision Council of your life, and she exercises her power with gusto. Your next holiday destination? Your next job? The length of your ties? When you get

to see your family? The name of the pet? (which was yours before you met her, anyway, but who names his dog Rocky? What a stupid name; we're calling him Pigcaso, because I love art, and he does look like a pig.) Do not forget the power of veto. No, you are not allowed to talk to your coworker Cynthia, because since she lost weight, she's a slut. She rules and manages your life with military discipline, and you, of course, humbly abide by her decisions. When you are at a party, she's the one who decides when to leave, and she even decides who your friend is and who's not anymore. Without even acknowledging your group of close friends has been replaced by hers. This is also a consequence of your crew getting tired of your constant rejection. Have you ever been at a restaurant and heard the following conversation between a married couples in their sixties?

Husband: "I'm so hungry, I think I'll have the tuna tonight. I have had a craving for seafood since this morning."

Wife: "No, you're not. They put too much garlic in it. I will be smelling your reeky mouth from the sofa to my bed all night."

Husband: "You're right, pumpkin. Maybe I'll just have the pasta with shrimp, then."

Wife: "That's what I'm having. Choose something else."

Husband: "The halibut sounds nice."

Wife: "You'll have the chicken piccata. And stay away from the asparagus. It makes you belch like a truck driver."

Husband: "Of course. I am sorry, pumpkin."

If you relate to the above example, you have reached the golden age in terms of pussy-whipped. An entire life of servitude and subjugation. Perhaps not; they may just be a happily married old couple who love each other. Your outlook on life matters, so which statement is right?

3. Finances: Your money is now "our" money. But hers is only hers. I have a friend who met another friend, and after some dating, they decided to get married. Since she's a economics major, she—not them—decided she would manage the family's finances. The matter turned a bit alarming—and unfair—when she began to receive alerts to her phone whenever a charge on his credit card was made; she would later reproach him. "Why did you buy a venti latte yesterday? You always get tall. Who the heck needs twenty ounces of coffee anyways? Don't you know we are tight on money this month?" She asked him to cut down on hobbies, clothing shopping, and other expenses because of their "insolvency"; while she, on the other hand, spent as much as she wanted, without giving an account to anyone.

    Most men in the pussy-whipped category take their paycheck to their partner for her to decide what do to with it. If you are an adult and have to request money from your partner, money that you earned, fair and square, that means you are pussy-whipped.

4. Reactions: You are always afraid of her reactions. Do you call your girl "muffin," "pumpkin," "sweet pea," or "angel" (my fave)? Any of the terms, most guys agree, deserve a punch in the face. You know you don't do it out of love, admiration, or tenderness, right? You do it in a feeble attempt to soften her reactions to everything you do that could anger her: let's say a guys' night out, you not being able to buy her that ring she wanted, or your inability to breathe more silently. Good news or bad news, the first thing that pops into your mind and makes your legs tremble is thinking about how she'll respond when she hears it. To the point, you even forget how this piece of news affects you.

    A guy once told me this interesting story: His cousin bought an engagement ring for his domineering girlfriend and decided to propose one night. They drove to their favorite spot—probably just hers—and he concealed the ring behind his back and began his speech, saying things like he had waited his entire life to meet his soulmate, how the sun shone for her, and so on; you get the gist.

The girl turned to him and said, "Are you proposing? Because that ring better be over ten thousand dollars, or I don't even want to see it."

He panicked and returned the ring back to his box; the ring, while beautiful, was less than ten thousand dollars. So next morning, the happy couple went to the store and replaced his shitty ring with one that muffin from hell approved of. For most women in love, a guy proposing is one of the happiest moments in their lives; for overly controlling women, though, the happy-level depends on the ring, whether the setting was perfect, and other things. And for pussy-whipped men, it all stands according to her reactions. Whop-eesh! (That's my favorite way of writing the sound of a lash, by the way.)

5. Your taste has magically changed:

- Clint: Yo, Kevin, I have tickets for the game tonight.
- Kevin: Really? I have to ask Emily if I can go. Hold on a minute. (Debate in the background)
- Kevin: Sorry, bro. Emily reminded me we have that potpourri workshop tonight. I forgot.
- Clint: What? Grow some balls, man.
- Kevin: It's not like that, Clint; you don't understand.

Before you met this girl, your idea of a perfect weekend was playing basketball Saturday morning, come home, and spend the rest of the afternoon watching reruns of *Lethal Weapon*. Sunday meant barbecuing with some friends and listening to Pearl Jam and Green Day (ah, the '90s). Of course, that's not the case anymore, because if you look at your calendar now, which your girl dutifully filled out for you, you realize you're going to a museum on Friday night. Her friend's cousin's ex-roommate is an artist, and he has an exhibit of his last work, titled *The Unbearable Misery of My 400-Thread-Count Sheets*. And of course, you must attend; you need to expose yourself to art and ultimately because she wants to go. Forget about shooting the hoops, and Martin Riggs fixing the world on Saturday; you are now going to have lunch with her mom and three sisters, to discuss details about some cousin's wedding in the country. No more barbecuing; no more Guns 'n' Roses. You now like Celine Dion, and the closest to rock you can hear at your place is Kylie Minogue. When your lady signs you up to affairs unbeknownst to you, without your permission, you, my friend, are whipped.

6. Errands: You are Cinderella now. "Make the fire, fix the breakfast. Wash the dishes, do the moppin' and the sweepin' and the dustin'" (such a catchy tune). You finally won a golden ticket to a guys' night out. Your crew is impressed and surprised, and as you drink a few beers and begin to relax, you all start to share anecdotes about your week. One of your friends landed a promotion, another one met a cute girl via Tinder who turned out to be his second cousin, and now it's your turn to announce your big news: You found a way to remove those stubborn stains from the sink using just baking soda and white vinegar. That's right. Because you are officially the maid. You wash and fold her thongs, you take out the trash, you do the dishes, and you mop the floor and ask her politely not to step on it while it's still wet ("Pretty please, angel; thanks for understanding"). And you volunteer to do her shopping. You finally understood the difference between carmine and rouge lip liners, and after several attempts, you found a toilet paper that doesn't irritate her bum. And what is the queen doing, while you run errands and sweat like a pig, cleaning the windows all the way to the top? She is relaxing, sitting in front of the TV, drinking a cocktail and waiting for her nails to dry.

7. Attention: You've turned into her BFF, the governor of Friend Zone. Pussy-whipped men do not have sex anymore; they seldom make love. Forget about seldom; I meant never. What are your boyfriend, spouse, or partner duties reduced to? Maybe, in the middle of the night, while she is out with her friends, while you peacefully sleep because your new bedtime is 10:30 p.m., she calls you desperately. She needs comforting because that wicked Samantha claimed her nose job was botched, in which case you

proceed to tell her that's not true, that her nose resembles Kate Beckinsale's, and by the way, her mouth is like a ripe strawberry in the spring. Maybe she got a flat tire, or she ran out of cash, or her left stiletto broke; at any rate, you dart out of your home to save your damsel in distress. Why? Why do you put up with her ingratitude? Because you secretly hope that all your heroic actions will turn Netflix night into an "action under the sheets" night, like in the good old days. Because you implore the seven heavens for her not to be tired, not in the mood, one of her special days (for the third time this month; talk about bad luck). Because you miss her, in all truthfulness, or at least the idea of being intimate with someone, and you wonder those weekend nights, since she goes out most of them, if she's seeing someone else. You've become her unconditional friend, the official receptor of her emotions (bad ones), and her own personal complaint department.

Guys are willing to comply with the most ridiculous requests from their women to please them; little whipping rituals, I would say. Like my friend who had to deliver a triple venti, half-sweet, nonfat, and caramel macchiato every single day at three o'clock to his girl, no matter the place, or otherwise the poor thing would have a headache. Another man needed to call and check up on his partner every night at ten o'clock. The guy could be in the middle of a meeting, making a speech, saving a baby from a falling streetlamp (remember that awesome scene from *Superman*?), but if that phone didn't ring by 10:05 am, boy. He was in deep trouble.

8. Independence: You are no longer an independent person. So now you have a joint mail account. And before you know it, you're "writing" emails to your friends, signed by both of you but authored by her. You may not have a joint account, but she knows the password to your email, your cell phone, your bank account, and your college website because she knows that Claire from Advanced Chemistry had a thing for you twenty years ago. I heard a story that I sort of hope was not true, about a man who was forced to buy his girlfriend an Xbox. Whenever he was playing,

she would join the group chat the whole time, without playing or actually participating, but to make sure he was actually playing and not partying without her. Have you ever been interrupted in the middle of a game, a meeting, or a trip by your woman, who demanded your immediate attention? You need to accept it, then; you are pussy-whipped. You're no longer in control your actions and your doings. Maybe you're not even allowed to control your thoughts; *deodamnatus* (that's Latin for "Damn it").

9. Friendless: Where have all the boys gone? Your friends don't even bother anymore. They stopped calling you, seeking you, trying to advise you. They got frustrated and angry every time they tried. Now you get nothing because everyone just assumes that you'll be kept under lock and key all weekend, and the sad thing is, they've given up trying to help you escape. You have become friendless. Damn, that's sad.

10. Your intuition: Lastly, these signs may seem alien to what you experience in your relationship. The truth of the matter is, you do not need a dominating girl who screens the texts you send out to prove you are pussy-whipped. It only takes your intuition to do so; you know it in your heart. You no longer feel funny, interesting, or even desirable, to her or to the world. Her power has emasculated you to the point of draining your identity and personality. Submission comes at a high cost, and sorrowfully you have no one to blame but yourself.

Five Types of Pussy-Whipped

Not all the whipping comes in the same form, and not all pussy-whipped men behave in the same manner. Below, I present to you five of the most common types of pussy-whipped men:

1. The PDA. This guy has his hands all over his partner 24/7, or maybe she has her leash—excuse me, her arm—around his neck all the time. He kisses her constantly, even in front of people, and says things like, "I'm so lucky to have you," while the rest of the guys feel their insides twist in a wave of nausea.

2. The hip-attachment. This annoying man brings his lady everywhere he goes: bowling night, bars, a reunion of his all-men club, his annual performance review at work, and so on. The dominatrix has to be present. Not only that, since a lady is present, you guys need to tone it down with the dirty jokes, the language, the drinking, and the locker room talk. Rally-killer.

3. The "my girlfriend." This guy, despite being pussy-whipped, keeps referring to his woman as "my girlfriend" and shoving this into every single conversation. You guys are talking about taking a backpacking trip? "Oh, coincidentally, my girlfriend went backpacking to Spain last year." Are you reminiscing about a memorable fishing trip? "You know what? My girlfriend's father has an impressive fishing boat." And he always needs to buy something for her. "Look at this. It so reminds me of my girlfriend. I better get her one."

4. The morally afflicted. Since the poor man is not allowed to have fun anymore, he feels a moral necessity to restrict the rest of you from doing what boys do. Even if his lady-boss is not around, and the crew starts talking about a celebrity (who gets offended by that?), the guy would say something like, "Come on, you guys, let's show some respect."

5. The denier. This guy refuses to admit his condition. He goes like this: "Stop calling me pussy-whipped. I am telling you I'm not. Cut it out. Oh, wait. I have a text from my girlfriend. I have to run; she needs a foot massage, and I know exactly how to alleviate her heel callouses. But I am telling you I haven't caved. I am not being whipped, for Pete's sake."

Now, since you are avidly reading this, you may be trying to learn from your mistakes, or you may be an ex-lady-boss attempting to mend whatever hell you put Josh through (you made him ask for your forgiveness on his knees in the middle of the movie theater. C' mon, anybody can confuse a Diet Coke with Coke Zero). Or you may be a wise person who likes to learn about relationships from every possible angle.

In every possible scenario, it is useful to determine the causes. What happened to this man and his masculinity, and his will, and his self-esteem? He was normal, until he met you.

Causes: What Happened?

The general theory of relationships says women are not attracted to insecure, feeble, pusillanimous men; on the contrary, Hollywood and mainstream pop culture encourage us to fall in love with the idea of a bad boy, from Danny Zuko to Tyler Durden to Khal Drogo (Oh, I would've learned Dothraki in a day for him). You know what I am saying, right? The general conception is supposedly that women are instinctively attracted to someone who does not necessarily treat them well. And the good guys get relegated to the Friend Zone. If this theory were 100 percent true, then why do women keep pussy-whipping their men? Why do men keep falling into this same trap?

The answer is not straightforward. But let's attempt to discover the reasons for the phenomenon through different theories:

a) Some guys are insecure. Picture this: a guy in his teens, suffering from severe acne that leaves marks in his face, but the scars in his persona are deeper. He was bullied, not popular, made fun of, called "geek" too many times. He reaches adulthood and is handsome, successful, and even rich. But inside, he's still the kid who played oboe in the school band as he tearfully watched his crush in the arms of that scumbag fullback at rugby games. He's all grown up now, but the same insecurities haunt him day after day. One night at happy hour, he meets Layla. Layla is cute, somewhat funny, with an acid tongue. Who cares? She's interested in him and actually wants to date him. He chooses to ignore that Layla can be quite mean because he finally found someone who wants to sleep with him. So they do; maybe even later, they get married. You can fill up the rest. Because every time Layla humiliates him, restricts sex to punish him, or anything of that sort of ghost from the past will remind him what it meant to be alone, what it meant to be a loser. And he makes a decision. It is better to be a loser with Layla than without her. So who cares if she's a little demanding? That's what relationships are about, aren't they?

Insecure men, for whatever reason (not necessarily because of high school reasons), tend to put up with this sort of behavior. Not because they consciously enjoy it, but because they seek attention like an abandoned puppy.

b) Conflict avoiders. My second theory states that men innately want to avoid conflict. Women, not so much. I mean, we've all been there, right? After a fight, you both drift apart; women take a shower and have a thousand mental conversations with themselves, ready to attack back, using examples, like his sister's stupid decision to buy a magenta vintage car, and we are prepared to cite Aristotle to prove our points. Men, on the other hand, go to the kitchen to make some tea and think about the discussion for about thirty seconds; they then proceed to focus on their bread and butter and begin wondering if butter is indeed healthier than margarine. They then remember their favorite show is on, and the conflict miraculously, if temporarily, vanishes from their head.

Generally speaking, men avoid conflict. And what is the best way to stay away from a fight? To comply and surrender to the other person's wishes, even if that means compromising your dignity, your money, and your favorite pudding that your grandmother made for you before passing away (Oh, she wants it? That's okay. It's not like the recipe was gone with her. It was? Oh, well. I have sweet memories instead then.). Don't get me wrong; it is indeed physically and mentally exhausting to be in conflict about everything. But these guys have simply given up, because acting against their women can mean fighting, losing them, or not being able to have sex. The way they see it is, wifey in a good mood means more sex for me. Happy wife, happy life. (Argh! Sorry to break it up for you, but this is not always the case.)

c) They think short-term. Let's say there was a happy couple; they are dating, and everything seems happy and sane. Then, boy screws up; girl gets mad. Boy apologizes, takes full responsibility for the blunder, and begs for a second chance. Girl likes that; she forgives him, and they move on. Time passes, and there's another fight. This time, boy was not to blame entirely, but he remembers the sweet reconciliation and how little it took for him to apologize, so he does it. Girl approves, and they move on. By the third time, even if the boy blinks in the wrong way, he will be conditioned to ask for forgiveness and mend his error. Men think short-term; they do not realize that by following this repetitive pattern, they have turned their relationship into a "dominatrix–submissive" one. They are unable to foresee how one repetitive act will turn into a way of living over time. Men love instant gratification, so for them, abstaining from complaining and always apologizing is a short, tiny step to be in peace. What they fail to see is that they are turning their women into hard-to-please monsters. A simple, lame apology is not nearly enough now; they want roses, and then money, and ultimately, yes, that sacred last piece of mouthwatering pudding that your nana made for you before leaving this world.

d) Men cannot be abused if they are the abusers. The last theory revolves about the fact that in our society, it is okay for a woman to say she was mistreated, submitted, and abused. But for a man to admit that, it's nearly impossible. Few men will admit it, and no one will believe those who do. It's like the tale of the Little Red Riding Hood; if you ask anyone who the villain is, they will all reply the Big Bad Wolf. Now let's say (significant spoiler ahead, if you haven't read it yet) that at his trial, the Big Bad Wolf admits guilt but also files a complaint against the hunter who caught him. He says his rights were violated, there was an unnecessary use of force against him, and he was called offensive names such as "Dog." Who would believe him? This guy has been terrifying the town for decades, and now he wants to appear as a victim? Give me a break. Right?

The same thing happens to men. First of all, recognizing nonphysical abuse is truly difficult for most people; now imagine if the abuser is said to be a woman. Men are taught, at a very young age, that they are stronger, designed to carry the world on their shoulders, and should not complain. Women do complain at a much higher rate than men do; surely they have centuries of history to back up their stories, but they can be the villains as well. And for those men who even dare to express it, society is ready to condemn them hastily. So what do they do? They shut up about it. They behave "like men."

Misconception of Other Men Being Called Pussy-Whipped

We have spent a fair amount of time discussing pussy-whipped men. So to give this negative side a rest, I want to talk a bit about the positive side. Yes, there is a bright side; call me an optimist, but I believe there is a pot of gold at the end of each rainbow, and I believe there is a beneficial side of men being considerate to their other half. They should not be seen as being pussy-whipped.

Regarding the above women's conduct, I do not agree with any of their acts. I think their behavior is disrespectful, mean, and entirely wrong. But I think the term has been unfairly utilized to describe the category of men who are loving, cooperative, and supporting partners. We, as a society, need to realize how absurd it is to make fun of someone for being attentive to their partner.

- Making your girlfriend, wife, partner your number one priority is not the worst thing in the world; it's what makes relationships last. Since the term is often used by men to call other men, let me explain it so you understand. Let's say you are at a sausage fest, and your girlfriend needs you for something important (not to rearrange the furniture at 11 p.m. on a Friday, because it is messing up her feng shui). What do you do? You leave, of course. She, the woman you decided to share your life with, needs your help.
- Making decisions together is not being submissive; it's called a partnership. Men say that when a guy lets his girl make important decisions, he is no longer a man. According to these parameters, a real man must be able to come and go as he pleases, without consulting her. A real man should be able to hang out with his boys and not answer to anyone about it, including his girl. So a good boyfriend or husband who sees his partner as an equal for everything is less of a man because of it? Let me remind you of

the centuries in which women lived submitted to their men's will; it's not like the roles have interchanged. What women want is equality, empathy, and understanding.

Yes, strong men shouldn't have to ask permission to eat a doughnut after 8 p.m. "because it makes you restless at night," but this should work both ways. If a woman wants to control his life, his calendar, and his wallet, you have every right to call him pussy-whipped. If the woman demands time, affection, and respect, and the guy complies, that's not succumbing; that is caring.

If we are still calling men whipped for choosing a committed relationship over a group of dudes who still get together every night to shoot darts and discuss high school issues ("I swear to you, dude, Camille Benson totally messed up Tony that summer. We had to stop giving him wedgies."), then we as a society have taken two steps back regarding maturity.

Issues of Being Pussy-Whipped

I think I've painted an ugly enough picture of the downside of being pussy-whipped. Here's a list of the cons of turning into one, in case you've forgotten:

- You lose your voice. If you're always told what to do, soon enough, your opinions on what you want are gone. There's no point in uttering the words; it's like talking to a wall when you are with your lady-boss.
- You will never meet her expectations, and her demands will increase over time. If you are with a person who is used to getting away with everything, who likes to being pampered, who is capricious, the sky's the limit when it comes to their demands. Don't kid yourself, thinking once you finally get her the car she wants, once you stop suggesting what to do on weekends, she will stop. On the contrary, her expectations will never be reached because she will want more from you each time.

- You will lose yourself. What's a person, anyway? Forgive me for throwing you a bit of philosophy here; people have ideas, thoughts, feelings, desires, plans, hobbies, preferences, friends. If you take that away, you reduce the person to an animal, to a group of cells arranged to survive, a body that needs to eat, sleep, and have an occasional milkshake (hell, yes; everyone needs a milkshake every now and then). So by giving up your dreams and aspirations to satisfy someone else's, you lose a vital part of yourself.

- You will eventually try to get even. This is the creepy "I told you so" portion no one wants to hear. I like this old saying: "There is no evil that lasts 100 years, nor a fool who endures it." The point is, no one, no matter how weak, stupid, feeble, insecure, blind, stubborn they are, will undergo a life of misery without eventually snapping and doing something about it. Now, I am not saying this is undesirable. Yes, you want that person to be free of his or her misery, and yes, you applaud the awakening. But you do not want to be in front of that person when the last drop of water fills up his glass, because he will explode.

Revenge is a dish that's best served cold. Months and months of punishment, mockery, humiliation, and ridiculous demands eventually catches up with you. And even the sweetest, most loving, and humblest people can turn into someone scary and unrecognizable if their partner pushes the wrong buttons.

Final Word

Up to this point, we've all assumed that the leading ladies of our horrid stories are heartless witches, and … they are (just kidding). What I am trying to say is, deep down, we all want to have a strong man by our side. Yes, we absolutely adore saying, "I told you so," when we are right ("For the nineteenth time, cousin Riley lives three blocks to the left, not to the right, honey"). And even after those small victories, deep down, we feel uncomfortable when we treat our partner like a child.

So unless you are hopeless and want to be with these kinds of men (or turn yours into one), there are some things we can do to actually help them. And the first thing we need to realize is that we are not the mothers of our boyfriends or husbands. It's hard for them to find the solution on their own; remember, men are simplistic. If they need to go from point A to point B, they will always choose the shorter, less stressful way. If that means coping with a lady-boss, then so be it.

A typical guy will want to come home from work and relax, have some peace and quiet, practice one of his hobbies, eat a nice dinner with you, and maybe later get some action. He does not want to come home to more drama, more demands, more yelling. If this means letting you be the boss, he'll do it.

But if he has reached that point where he no longer wants to argue, where he will say yes so you stop yelling, you may think you have won. But in reality, you have lost; because he has given up on you and the relationship.

So how do you fix it? How do you rewind? Easy: stop! Stop controlling him, stop bossing him, and stop parenting him. Need more of an explanation? Here are a few pointers:

1. Stop planning for him. This translates into no searching jobs for him, no contributing to a more successful career, no planning your wedding before he's ready to talk about it.
2. Stop making him feel like he's always in trouble. He is not a little boy, and he is undoubtedly not your puppy (even if his mamma named him "Bubo"; for Pete's sake, he's a human being.), so stop treating him like one. Like he needs to be punished for a no-no he did in the kitchen last night. And while we are on this, he is not the official receptor of all your emotions. Learn to get a grip. Yes, he is yours, but he's not your confessor or your kindergarten teacher.
3. Stop criticizing his hobbies, job, passions, or friends, especially in public. If you chose this man to be your partner, you have to admire him and like him for what he is. If not, break it off. But do not try to change someone to accommodate your taste. Show some respect for what he wants and the way he wants to obtain it.
4. Last but not least, give him space. Set him free. That doesn't mean he can come and go as he pleases. It means to trust him to have some time off without saying this will be bad for the relationship. People need a day off, to have a beer, to hang out with friends. We all do.

In conclusion, there comes the point in a man's life when he wants to be serious with a girlfriend or partner. If that's you, congratulations; you have reached a milestone. One suggestion: Don't screw this up. It doesn't happen to everyone, trust me. No one wants to be a slave, and you shouldn't be proud to be the boss, either. None of these roles make anyone happy in the long term. Work as a couple, talk about your issues, and take a step back if you need to. If nothing else works, break up. As the saying goes, "Stop looking for happiness where you lost it."

Chapter 2

DICK-WHIPPED

My cousin and her husband were going through a rough streak in their marriage. He didn't appreciate her efforts to keep the marriage afloat. She suggested everything from couple's therapy to a visit to a local shaman (call me crazy, but the guy totally cured my phobia of elbows. What? They are odd-looking, purposeless, and get wrinkly over time.) Anyways, she was willing to try everything, while he, on the other side, claimed the relationship was doomed, and it was basically a matter of time before the divorce was set on the table. One day, I came over to her house early in the morning, and she was diligently making breakfast … for him. Now, I'm not talking about instant coffee and some PB&J over toast; no, the woman was preparing freaking eggs Benedict, cutting fresh fruit, and brewing coffee.

I, of course, asked her, "Why are you all Julia Child-like at 7 a.m.?"

Without stopping poaching eggs, she hastily said, "Vincent [the devil in disguise] has an early meeting today; he asked for Béarnaise sauce, but silly oh me forgot to buy shallots or peppercorns. So I asked him if hollandaise sauce was okay. Can you help me beat those egg yolks?"

I couldn't believe it. This man had publicly announced their marriage was over, and he had refused to try to mend things up between them; he was probably seeing another woman. Please. Who needs to meet with their "accountant" on a Saturday evening and then spends the night because the paperwork was endless? Yet he had the nerve to ask for some freaking eggs Benedict from her. More astoundingly, she was willing to comply. Why?

Why in the name of all good, sweet, and pure of this world, including Adam Levine and cream cheese, would she behave that way? Because she was being dick-whipped.

This informal term describes what happens when a girl becomes obsessed with her man and lets him control her life. This rather emotional state turns a woman crazy; she's inexplicably attached to her man to the point of enduring his physical or psychological abuse. No matter how he treats her or how much he uses her, she still wants to be with him. If you haven't experienced this yourself (you go, girl!), you've probably seen it elsewhere. Successful, attractive, hot ladies yielding to an unappreciative, abusive, good-for-nothing guy. What's in it for them? Sex. These ladies are devoted to his lovemaking.

Most women are aware of their man's filthy habits: They drink, they're abusive, they cheat shamelessly, and yet, they come home every day at six o'clock to dinner waiting on the table. Are these women martyrs? You have this dutiful woman, like my cousin, serving him dinner, eating peacefully with him. Does she have dignity? Yes, but even better, she has a plan, a plan to guilt him so he finally feels remorseful, gives up his filthy habits, and improves his bad manners. She sees the picture in her head: He will eventually feel guilty and give up; he'll be devoted to his long-suffering wife. Persistence is the answer to her problems, the key to happiness. He will go through the emotional tunnel; he just needs a kick. But will he? Go figure.

Do the following extracts sound familiar?

"Did you know Christy's husband hit on the kids' teacher the other day?"

"Please, the man jumps on everything that has a pulse."

"I don't understand. She knows he cheats and lies but doesn't do anything about it. Why?"

"Because she is dick-whipped."

"Lily, are you ready? The movie starts in forty-five minutes. I'll pick you up in fifteen."

"Can I take a rain check? I can't make it."

"What? Why? It was your idea."

"Mmmm, turns out I have to check on Rob's reservations, pack his suitcase, and go over his presentation for tomorrow."

"WTF? Why can't he do it?"

"He went for a run."

"OMG. I cannot believe it. You are so dick-whipped."

"What? No. It's not like that; he went to blow off steam. You don't understand."

Even though the bad guy in these scenarios is the guy, duh! Who's really to blame? Who, ultimately, is willing to accept this kind of behavior? You.

This isn't about trash-talking a particular man (although that can sometimes be quite fun), but we must analyze you. What makes you prone to attract men who are no good for you, who use you and maltreat you? To this point, your relationship status doesn't even matter; if you are married, living together, dating, if you've ever let a man control your life for an extended period, you are dick-whipped.

Why are you letting him do that, girl? (See? The comma here is crucial. Otherwise, you would be asking, why are you letting him do that girl? That's a valid question. If he's supposed to be doing only you.)

You know the saying: fool me once, shame on you. Fool me twice, shame on me. Who is ultimately to blame? The woman who is forced to turn to a sperm bank because the guy won't perform in the bedroom? Is it considered cheating if she is forced to use a vibrator? Is fantasizing about the guy next door wrong? How can she ever feel aroused if she has no memories to feel great about?

You are working double shifts to make ends meet and so your eye-candy can pursue his career as a "Bacon-critic" (I didn't make this up, this job actually exists, and before you apply, I have to say it's quite competitive). You see the bags under your eyes, you realize you haven't had a pedicure in ages, your feet resemble Frodo's, and you feel tired and overwhelmed. This is not the life you envisioned for yourself. But you know what? It doesn't matter to you. Because you repeat a mantra that keeps on going: "He wants me. That incredible, handsome, smart, witty man is mine." And everything else loses significance. And if arguing with a guy madly in love is difficult, debating with an obsessed woman is as hard as climbing Mt. Everest on one foot. Women who are irremediably in love are like a dog that won't release its bite; they won't budge. There's no leeway. Only their side of the story counts.

And while that mantra says, "He wants me," reality keeps screaming at them, "He isn't worth it!"

Before we get all physiological, quoting from Freud to Pavlov to Dr. Phil, it doesn't matter if you had a bizarre relationship with your father. Or if Timmy from junior summer camp treated you awfully (damn you, Timmy; you showed my diary to everyone). Or if you grew up in an all-female environment and your social skills were truncated. The thing is, you cannot differentiate between a good catch and a scumbag because no one taught you how. You are prosperous, popular, gorgeous, and funny, but you are also naïve; you will stumble against bad guys 80 percent of the time you try to date. That's a statistic most of us would like to ignore (and probably why we think fairy tales are much better than reality). According to studies, most women will end up with men who mistreat them.

You can argue that your case will be different because your man pursued you for years; therefore, this has to be the real thing. Or that you finally gave your best friend a shot after all the begging and endless carnation bouquets. I don't mean to break your heart, but even then, once the guy fulfills his fantasies, once he declares himself your "pussy major," once he learns how to take the most advantage of you, well, he will.

That's right: eight out of ten men you meet are worthless (you're welcome, by the way).

What's the challenge? Where's the hope? The aspiration, my friends, is to find those two men out of ten. The keepers, the ones worth the shot. The ones who will not break your heart or use you. You think it's easy? Try telling that to a celebrity like Elizabeth Hurley, gorgeous, hot, popular, desired, who gets cheated on by, um, Hugh Grant? Now, I'm not saying that celebrities are perfect by any means; Lord knows they are not exactly worth the National Medal of Merit, but they easily prove my point. CEOs, top athletes, world leaders get used and abused by their romantic partners. They struggle, like you and me.

Now, if I said I had a special formula, or a magic wand, to let you know if that guy you're having some cocktails with is a piece of shit or Prince Charming, would you use it? Would you really like to know?

The answer, of course, is no. You don't want to know. You're fed up with this nonsense, but you embrace it nonetheless.

Years ago, I went to a funeral. The deceased was the father of an acquaintance, and I had heard he wasn't exactly faithful. Not only that, my friend's mom was the one who supported him via a successful career in real estate. Anyways, we were in the middle of the tears and sobs when two other families showed up. That's right; he was not only cheating on her, but he also had two entire other families, with kids and everything. So technically, there were three widows howling over this guy.

I was in shock and wondered what my friend's reaction would be (and his mom's). But nothing prepared me for it, because when the ceremony was over, the mom began defending him, saying, "Who the hell do these other ladies think they are? They had no respect for the original" family." Remember, this woman had no idea of the existence of these women and children. Nonetheless, she dashed against them.

Your age, looks, financial status, or level of education will not spare you from being dick-whipped. It is also not a matter of luck. It is a matter of mind-frame and willingness to see reality as it is. It is also a matter of self-esteem; no fully secure woman falls for this. If this has happened to you—or currently is—there's something unhealed in you; a crack in your heart or something. And when these guys notice it, perceive it, boom; you're doomed. Because if there's something that men love more than a remote control, and a double Western bacon cheeseburger, it's having control over weak women. (We're still talking about the eight out of ten men, not about Jack from *Titanic*: "If you jump, I jump.")

So go ahead and think you've never fallen for it. Lie to yourself and say you are smarter than any other of those other women. Now, when you're in bed and about to close your eyes, be honest and remember when you let that bad boy sweep you off your feet like a teenage girl. And you welcomed this sort of spell, with a naïve, open heart and an eager desire down there. You know why? Because it feels awesome. Like a thousand lips kissing you, while you eat full-fat ice cream, at Disneyland. Passion is like a drug; you can ask any of those poor addicts why they do it. Their answer won't be complicated. They will merely say because it feels fucking awesome. And since you've tasted a piece of heaven, you'll do anything to get it back if you've lost it. Boom. You're dick-whipped.

Here are the most common reasons why women fall this heavily for scumbags or bad boys:

- We see potential in them. So when we say, "bad boys," we mostly picture James Dean on a motorcycle with a cigarette clenched between his perfect teeth and a look in his eyes that says "You're mine." Before you start defending your man, saying, "My Otto is nothing like that. He has a PhD and has class," let me break it to you: If your Otto lives off you, refuses to commit, is selfish in bed, orders you to cook and clean after him, I don't care if he's working on a cure for cancer; he's a scumbag. Call it maternal instinct or naivety; there's an innate desire in women to make our men a better version of themselves. Like exploiting their true potential, even if there's no potential to begin with. I'm sure you know women who support their partners when they are aspiring artists ("I swear, Monica, my next book will be a hit; it's about how wearing a watch actually steals time away from us") or misunderstood scholars ("Nobody gets me, Elodie; while others chit-chat, I observe. I rationalize. I'm probably the smartest guy in every place we go.") or, of course, the eternal boy with emotional issues ("It's not you, Chloe. I just don't know how to be a boyfriend. I wasn't made for love, maybe because no one ever loved me."). Different scenarios, same premise: We believe our love, patience, devotion, submission, and obedience will solve our guy's issues, whatever they are. And then, once he's happy, once we help him reach his goals, unleash his creativity, conquer that business, learn how to love, we will by his side and live happily ever after.

What's wrong with wanting to help your man improve? Nothing. But it's one thing to help each other reach their dreams and another thing to solve someone else's life. If your guy has a significant problem, it's up to him to acknowledge it and then fix it or get help. How can you tell if you're doing this? Well, if you meet someone and immediately have a checklist of things you would change, then you're unequivocally betting on the relationship based on an unrealistic expectation.

- Passion. Oh, you greatest deceiver. Passion makes us believe that that guy who shoved you into the coat closet in the middle of your Aunt Deborah's sixtieth birthday, because he just had to have you right there, is in love with us. Bad boys are known to be passionate, and women either enjoy the ride or think they'll be able to tame them. You can't blame a woman for dreaming about this; by taming a bad boy and turning him into a good boyfriend, you're having Mark Darcy and Daniel Cleaver in one single package. Isn't that the dream? Movies and TV series fill women's heads with the same idea: having deep conversations about life, scorching kisses, fingers interlocked while a wave of passion travels your body. Even the thought of forbidden love looks excellent on TV, but passion, while enticing, is short-lived.

- Personal issues or seeking for approval. Here comes the shrink's take on this: If a woman had trouble with the father figure in her life (perhaps he was absent, abusive, distant, or manipulative), she may subconsciously be looking for someone exactly like him.

- The innate desire to reproduce. You may say you don't want kids, which is totally fine. You may even gag at the thought of spending long nights burping a small human being and changing diapers; again, comprehensible enough. But there's a switch inside you that is not easily turned off; it's called the "desire to procreate." And that thing that you ignored in biology class (because you were passing notes with Alice about Clem being a total jerk) is what makes your hormones crazy. And don't get me started on what crazy hormones can make a woman do: from yelling at an alarm clock ("You were supposed to wake me up at seven, you stupid, useless thing") to pursuing a relationship with a man who seems like the best choice to father your offspring.

Signs of Being Dick-Whipped

As abuse comes in different forms and shapes, guys have a variety of reasons behind it. A guy may use his partner just for sex, with no commitment. This is so common and obvious, I would venture to say it's somehow avoidable. The matter gets trickier when we are talking about someone in a relationship, perhaps a boyfriend or a spouse who uses his partner for money or merely to boost his ego.

In this case, it is harder to recognize the signs. Let's start with the most important thing: how you actually feel. If you often feel bad about yourself or believe you're not enough, then you should take that as a hint that something is wrong.

Here are the most obvious signs you are being dick-whipped:

- He depends on you financially.

A friend told me this story: This girl met a guy, and they started going out. She was a successful dentist, and he was an entrepreneur (translation: he hasn't figured what to do in life and attempted a few, unsuccessful small businesses). After a while, she became pregnant, and since she was making more money than he was—he was actually not earning anything and lived off her—she was to pay all baby expenses until he got back on his feet. A small detail I haven't mentioned: He had already impregnated a different woman a few years back. And the same story kind of repeated itself, only this time, the mother of his first child required him to take on some responsibility for the girl, and he was to pay for things like school and medical insurance. So since this guy had nothing to offer, he had the nerve (I still have trouble digesting it) to ask his new girlfriend for money to give his-ex-girlfriend. And she accepted. She was working her ass, day and night, cleaning people's teeth to provide for her child, her useless boyfriend, and her boyfriend's ex-girlfriend's five-year-old girl.

There's nothing wrong in sharing expenses, or picking up the tab every now and then at a restaurant, especially when you know your partner is not doing well financially. That is way different than having a leech for a partner, sucking on you desperately so he can pay rent, food, and hobbies ("Honey, you know I have to change my hockey gear every six months. Should I put it on the credit card or can you give me cash?"). If he lives with you, if he doesn't have a job, or if his career doesn't cover his basic needs, then you are 100 percent being used.

No woman should provide financial responsibility to a man. Let me rephrase that: No person should be responsible financially for another, unless they are related. Most of us have enough on our plate already. Why would you work hard from nine to five to spend your precious money on a lazy guy who's unable to treat you like you deserve?

• He's a selfish lover.

Okay, I said earlier that bad boys are usually passionate and well qualified in the lovemaking department. (No, not because they have the *Titanic* Heart of the Ocean down there.) And the term "dick-whipped" indeed refers directly to a woman who, for the sake of continuing to have intercourse with this man, accept all kinds of abuse. But passion is fleeting, and even if when it's not, it can be unbalanced. Have you ever felt you're the one pleasing him in bed and getting nothing in return? That whole common belief that says that men are selfish in bed by default is bullshit. It is gratifying to receive pleasure, but it is also fantastic to give it. Real men love making their partners enjoy sex; they want to please them.

I heard a sad story about a girl. She had been in a relationship with this guy for over nine months. He was "perfect," she said to her friends, until one night, after a couple of tequilas, she began asking her closest friends about their sex sessions. You know, necessary inquiries: frequency, duration, partner rating, and so on; nothing gross like length or girth. Then she spilled the beans. So this guy made her go down on him for around half an hour, before he even touched her. She said, "At first I was flattered; I must be so good at it he has to experience it each time. Then I began to feel neglected. Don't get me wrong; the first five minutes are rewarding and fun. The next ten, I feel like a machine, and the last ten, my whole face is so numb I can only keep awake by analyzing which *Star Wars* movie was better and why. Then, we finally do it. And it lasts around two minutes. Of course, he's all done, satisfied and happy, and I'm still debating between *Battle of the Clones* and *The Empire Strikes Back*."

Can you believe this guy? And his excuse: "I get nervous sometimes." Oh, please.

• He always needs something from you.

Is your partner always borrowing your most prized possessions? And then returning them in bad shape? Your car, your TV, your friends? (Okay, that last one is a whole different subject.) So your guy believes you have opened a charity center uniquely designed to attend Mr. Poor Helpless Baby's needs on demand. Wrong.

Agreed, relationships are about sharing and receiving, and lending your stuff to your man sounds completely reasonable, until is not. These guys are always in trouble and in need of your help. But when it comes to them reciprocating, they are nowhere to be seen. From cooking and cleaning to doing his job to passing him the remote and a beer because "Baby, you are already standing up, and I am already on the couch." Analyze this carefully. Is he too reliant on you?

Maybe you notice he only pays attention to you or calls you when he needs something: sex, his shoes polished, money, a ride; you name it. And he keeps asking and asking. You know why? Because you keep giving and giving.

- He's seeing someone else.

A room. A couple is watching TV. The girl is watching the movie, but the guy keeps checking his phone. He chuckles now and then. The girl begins to feel uncomfortable and casually asks, "What's so funny, Brad?"

Brad immediately turns his phone, facing down and clears his throat. "Nothing. Victor sent some silly meme. It cracked me up."

"Oh? Let me see it."

"Um. Err … I erased it."

"Why are you being weird?"

"What do you mean? I'm normal, Jul … Kelly."

"Did you just call me 'Jules'? Who is Jules?"

"Geez, you're the one being weird. I'm going out for a bite. Don't wait up, okay?"

"Brad, don't go. I'm sorry. Let's just watch the movie, okay? Brad?"

Unless you are clinically paranoid, if you suspect your man is cheating on you, he probably is. If you consistently catch him lying, if he makes lame excuses for not being somewhere or leaving earlier, if he's suddenly vague about his whereabouts, he's dipping his pen in another woman's inkwell.

Why in the world would you put up with someone like him? It's hard enough to hold on to a relationship when the two parts are 100 percent committed, but when there's another figure in the picture, it makes it impossible. And humiliating for you.

I've heard many stupid excuses about why women put up with their partner's infidelity: "He can have a hotdog elsewhere, but he'll always return for his steak" (for you vegetarian and vegan readers, that means that guys can have trashy girls just for fun, but they always return home for the real thing). Another one: "It was a mistake, he apologized, and I love how he accepts his imperfections." No, woman. Imperfections are when a guy won't put his dirty clothes inside the basket or thinking Avril Lavigne represents '90s rock. But to taint your relationship with infidelity, to use you and lie to you about it, that's unforgivable.

- He's got a bad rep, and your friends warned you about it.

Sometimes, friends and moms can detect something you may be overlooking. With your parents, it may be because they've lived longer than you or they love you so much they pay attention to certain details.

Have you ever been with a guy who your friends don't like, and even his own friends warn you about him? Did you listen to their advice? If we're talking about his friends, and you refuse to acknowledge what they are trying to tell you, you are toast. These people know him in ways you don't or ever will; how can you ignore the fact that even they think you shouldn't go out with him?

True, rumors sometimes are just that: gossip. But the vast majority of time, they carry a piece of truth within. So before telling your loved ones to fuck off and mind their own business, try to put yourself in their situation. You have a friend who is funny, beautiful, successful, and can whistle *Don't Stop til You Get Enough*: a real keeper. And you see this gorgeous, amazing woman going out with a douchebag, a guy who uses her, depends on her financially, and on top of it, cheats on her. Wouldn't you want to shake her until she came to her senses? Well, think about that the next time your mom organizes an intervention to talk about your beau.

Dos and Don'ts of Being Dick-Whipped

Aren't we the masters at finding the silver lining of everything? Because even if you strongly believe nothing good can come out of being dick-whipped, you still can learn. And experiencing and absorbing life lessons merely is priceless.

- Do learn about your bad habits and issues. The first time, it will probably take you off-guard, but if you are a repeat offender and keep going after more mistreatment and abuse, you will eventually hit bottom. I am by no means telling you this is desirable, but nothing sets us back in reality like a good crash. And after that, the soul-searching begins, a catharsis to understand, accept, and work on your bad habits and issues with men. It's like having a nonhealthy relationship with chocolate. Your friends are worried and warn you, but you refuse to accept that five innocent bars per day are harmful. But then, they turn into seven, and by next month, you are eating ten bars of Toblerone each day until you get sick. I mean really ill, end up in the hospital, and swear you'll never touch chocolate again. But your conscience knows better; the chocolate has never been the problem, but the way you abused it and the reasons behind it were. You start digging, and eventually, you'll find the answers.
- Don't regret it. You will have experienced fun while it lasted. I'm not an advocate for regrets; what's done is done. And whatever you did, you did it because at the time, it seemed like the best option available (like when you picked that insane Japanese tattoo, but once it was on your skin, you learned what it really meant: skin rash). So there's no point in grieving over last time because let's face it: despite the drama and the bad moments, you had your fun with your bad boy.
- Don't try to change him. Please, oh, please, ignore your motherly instincts this time around and just accept you will not change this man. And even if he eventually changes (some actually do) and turns into someone worth it, your relationship has already been poisoned. Or even less than that, he's not willing to settle with you. The sooner you accept that Hollywood endings are fake, the faster you'll cope with reality and find a genuine way of being happy.
- Don't be fooled. Use and abuse come disguised in charming ways; we've covered that. An adventurous spirit, a rebellious soul,

an out-of-the-ordinary person is alluring, no doubt about it. Unfortunately, the package comes with defects as well, and these souls are often paired with the worst when it comes to relationship material. We have to be coherent with what we want. You can't ask a free spirit to be committed and monogamous; you can't expect an idealist, protesting on the streets, to be financially responsible. So set your priorities right.

Conclusion

When it comes to love, we've been taught to idolize intense, passionate relationships that truly hide a controlling, abusing behavior behind them. I'll give you that these are hard to spot. From *Romeo and Juliet* to *Twilight*, we have absorbed centuries of thinking love is all about a mindless obsession. Poems and songs have meddled into your mind and taught you if you really love someone, then you have to be willing to give it all, no questions asked. And when you translate everything to our days, to real life, turns out we are in reality describing a controlling, abusive man who dick-whips his partner.

Let's go back to the beginning. We've analyzed two things: how these scumbags do what they do, and signs you've become a victim. The information is in your hands; you have the power now. (Are you suddenly picturing Beyoncé, Tina Turner, or Serena Williams breaking her racket?) So what are you going to do about it? That's the real question.

Are you going to a) keep ignoring the facts and wasting your life and time with someone who does not deserve you, b) pretend this never happened to you, while deep down you feel mistreated, or c) take matters into your own hands and stop being victimized by men just because of their dick.

Remember the mantra you said to yourself every morning to put up with this abuse? "He's worth it. He wants me. He's great." How about changing it for: "I am worth it. I deserve better. I am too good for him." And give the mirror a good long look, because along with saying goodbye to this pathetic relationship, you are saying forever goodbye to the old you, the dick-whipped.

Chapter 3

DADDY'S DADDY, MUMMY'S BABY

"Honey, the kids are finally asleep. Netflix and chill sound good?"

"Oh! Yes, please. Do we have any popcorn?"

"Regular butter or feeling adventurous? I think chipotle-flavored popcorn is just the brightest idea anyone had after toilet paper. Honey?"

"Hold on. My dad is texting me. Shoot. We have to cancel our plans. I need to get home ASAP."

"What? What's wrong?"

"He needs the bathroom light bulb changed."

"I can't believe it. Why can't he change it by himself?"

"Show a little consideration, Becca; he is far from being young."

"Oh, so he's too old to change a freaking bulb but not too old to bang that busty bimbo from the golf club?"

"That's completely uncalled for. I need to go home."

"You are unbelievable, Tom. And by the way, I thought *this* was home."

I know what you are thinking: No way this scenario is a real-life example. No way could someone act that way. Unfortunately, and with genuine heartache, I can assure you two things: first, this happened to someone I know, and second, Becca ended up binging on chipotle popcorn watching *Dark*, and yes, both are a godsend.

You may have heard of people being called a "Mama's boy" or "Daddy's girl"; in both cases, parents continue to treat their children as toddlers. My friend's mom combs his hair by licking her hand and running it through his head. Ew! Okay, I'll stop the rambling. So this is entirely different. Here, an odd, bizarre, eerie relationship between a parent and a child takes place. What's the difference? The parents don't want to care for their son or daughter; they want to be taken care of by them.

Now, there is no particular term to describe this behavior; therefore, I proudly present the term I coined: "Daddy's daddy." Catchy, right? Okay, I'll admit it. There is a psychological term to define this behavior; it is called emotional incest or surrogate spouse syndrome. Doesn't Daddy's daddy sound so much better?

I am sure in terms of a son being attached to his mom, the term Mama's boy is familiar to everyone. There are also Mama's girls.

Going back to Daddy's daddy, why did I brilliantly come up with it? Well, think about it. In these relationships, the father wants to control his son and occupy the place in his life usually reserved for a romantic partner. It's like your boyfriend or husband is having an affair with his dad (sorry for the involuntary images popping in your head).

Parents have a crucial role in our lives. First, they keep you alive during your baby years by feeding you, taking you to the doctor, and of course, keeping you from eating the Christmas lights. They were in charge of your education; they covered your basic needs and, ultimately, turned the world into a warm, secure place for you to develop. A great deal of who we are as adults is directly linked to the efforts of our parents.

Reciprocating that love and protection is a natural, desirable thing once we are grown up and they grow old, especially in the case of parents with health issues, physical impairments, financial trouble, or otherwise.

And while I sound all mature and clever, let me assure you I am going somewhere; I do have a point. It is one thing to care for your daddy or mommy (and please stop calling them that once you're old enough to order an Alabama slammer) and another one to treat them as babies or (here comes the ew factor again) a romantic partner. The foundation of all evil resides in the extremes. Being loving and caring is a great thing; being cold and distant is not. Being overly attached and clingy is as bad as being aloof. Equilibrium is what we want. Yes, you do want to take care of your parent, but there is a limit to it.

No matter the circumstances, no matter the context, one should never become your dad's daddy or your dad's partner in life. It is unhealthy, damaging, and ultimately, sick.

Recognizing this type of behavior is not easy. The most common situation involves a codependent, controlling, meddling parent, usually the father, but it runs both ways (and a son or daughter too blind to face the truth). These sons and daughters neglect their personal lives, partners, and families to please their demanding parents. How can you spot this conduct?

Signs and Symptoms

Let us hear Bradley's desperate story:

> For over fifteen years, I had a great marriage. Surely we faced the occasional crisis, like every other married couple we know, but we managed to overcome them and continue to be happy. Almost three years ago, we received some unexpected, devastating news: Karen's mother became seriously ill. She and I discussed this for a while and decided to move near my in-laws so we could help out. Since Karen is the only daughter, it all made sense to me. Two years after we moved, her mother unfortunately lost her battle with cancer and passed away. And along with that, I have now lost Karen, my wife, to … her father! She has become, I wouldn't call her daddy's girl precisely, something between a mother and a wife to my father-in-law.

> Right after my mother-in-law became ill, her husband retired and took care of her. He has always been intelligent, filled with energy and strong-willed. He has also been a controlling person, ever since I've known him, and even though we used to live three towns apart, he attempted to meddle in our family decisions all the time. Now that

we live close to him, and since he is a widower, he wants to run the show.

He needs to get a say on everything: from the toys we buy for our kids, to the utility company we use, to the brand of cereal we get. He is a control freak who has gone far enough to tell us how to manage our relationship. The worst part? Karen, my wife, does not see the harm at all! She is oblivious to the amount of leverage her father has over her life. We are talking about a woman who is the branch director of a major corporation! Still cannot confront her dad. It's like she feels guilty or sorry about her father being alone, or wants to show appreciation for everything he has done for her. Either way, he is destroying our relationship, all with "his best intention at heart." When my mother-in-law was alive, she acted as a buffer against him; now that she is gone, he has unleashed his true self. I don't know what to do.

Before moving to the list of signs you should be aware of, let me flip the sides a little bit. Here's the other side of the story: a man being controlled by an overly demanding father:

My husband and I live far from our parents. On Christmas, since my firstborn was only a couple of months old, we decided to invite both families with us, to have a chance to spend an occasion with everyone. To my dismay and my family's, the minute my father-in-law entered my home, he started giving his opinions on how I was raising my baby wrongly, and how much I was neglecting my husband, his son, since I became a mother.

My husband's family comes from a different background, and my father-in-law is very traditional. He is accustomed to women staying home to tend their husbands and children; I have a full-time job, same as my husband, so that was his first cultural shock. The differences between his way of thinking and mine cause constant tension. He expects life to revolve around him; he wants to decide everything when we are together, what to eat, where to go, how much to spend. I get exasperated, while my husband remains quiet. And the situation permeates to my children too. While he loves them, his main focus is to spend time with his son. As if he was trying to make up for the time lost when he was little. While his intentions are good, his way of doing it is both disturbing and weird. I feel he has developed an unhealthy obsession towards my husband.

When we are alone, my husband and I have a wonderful relationship, and we can talk about everything. However, the moment my father-in-law shows at our doorstep, it turns my husband into a four-year-old, seeking his father's approval.

I feel torn most of the time because I do want my children to experience this side of their cultural heritage; I want them to get along with my father-in-law. But at the same time, I cannot approve of his behavior. Moreover, he shows little interest in them unless my husband is present, then he seems like the most caring grandfather. His manipulations have gone over the limit, and my husband either refuses to see it or wants to avoid conflict at all cost. I am just sick and tired of the situation.

Heartbreaking? Irritating? Infuriating? All of the above, right? By the way, no one should be allowed to talk to a sleep-deprived, first-time mother, also a wife, unless to say something like "Hand me the wailing yet precious and beautiful baby and go take a nap." Or "Here is a dozen of those cream cheese-filled doughnuts you like. Of course, breastfeeding requires carbs, and you do look amazing." Anything else? Just zip it.

So these parents are overly controlling and demanding. They are usually quite clever and utilize tactics that can be obvious or super subtle.

Ripping the bandage off your eyes is never easy. I know. But this list will give you an idea of how much your parent is trying to control you:

- They attempt to isolate you from your own family, your spouse/partner, or your friends. They are jealous of the time you spend with them. Here's a quick example: I have a friend whose husband's father passed away. He's the eldest son and has become a weird mixture of a partner and father to his mom. My friend and her hubby reached an agreement to spend the holidays for one year with his mom, and the next one with her family. When it's my friend's turn, her mother-in-law always makes a big deal. She says things like, "Oh, are you sure it's not my turn this year? Gee, I get to be all alone, while you guys go elsewhere. Maybe you should spend it again with me." Before you feel completely bad for her, let me tell you she doesn't spend the holidays alone; she has three more children. Plus, she never bathes her terrier. Okay, this last thing has nothing to do with it. But seriously, that poor thing is a walking, barky knot. My point is, she loves to play the victim with my friend's husband. She wants to be the center of attention all the time and make her son feel guilty about it.
- They violate your privacy. Flashbacks from your teen years? ("Mom! Can you please knock? And I was only looking at the pretty girls.") Privacy has now become a privilege in our digital era. Your phone spies on you, your computer is videotaping you, Facebook reads your mind (I'm serious; how the heck did Mark Zuckerberg know I was thinking about buying a new vacuum?). But your loved ones should be the first ones to respect you. Well, these parents know little about boundaries. They can check your phone, enter a room without knocking, call your boss to see how are you performing, suggest a different brand of underwear ("I swear to you, these briefs let your things breathe much better, Sonny"), give you advice on contraception, and the list can go on. And with that violation of your privacy, they violate the privacy of your partner too. Nothing stops them. They show up unannounced, give unrequested advice, and ask things that are just not their business.
- They blackmail you. Oh, some parents love playing the victims; they do it to get their children's attention, money, or time. "If I

had some money of my own, I wouldn't have to live in this lousy house." They also use guilt to get their way: "I spent twenty hours in labor to bring you into this life, and you can't spend a couple of hours with your mother?" or "I sacrificed my entire life, working hard to give you the best, and this is how you pay me?" Some more disturbing behaviors include the extra scoop of threatening: "If you don't come right now, I swear I will hurt myself. That's fine; leave me. Maybe I won't be alive tomorrow."

Let me tell you something real quick: You did not ask to be brought into this life. You did not request your parents to make you. In fact, your dad was certainly not thinking of you in the process. He was joyfully celebrating Valentine's and acting in consequence of a couple of margaritas and some slow dancing (and your mother's ultra-sexy bell-bottom pants, or was it just my parents?). Yes, they did the honorable thing and kept you alive and happy for the next eighteen years, but even so, you are not supposed to be their slaves. And you certainly are not to blame if they hurt themselves.

Conditional love is not true love. You cannot say, "If you love me, you must …" Fill in the blank: move in with me, name your daughter after me ("Sorry, Mom, I'm not naming my baby girl Veraminta."), break up with your partner, choose this career, cut your hair differently, and so on. If your father or mother set conditions, blackmailed you, or anything of that sort to make you prove your love and devotion, you have turned into a Daddy's daddy or Mommy's hubby.

Now, we've discussed the signs to spot disturbing behavior on their side. But there is something more important: How do you feel about it? And this is not only important because you matter and you are being aggravated here; it matters because it may be difficult to recognize their flaws. But it may be easier to identify how you feel toward the relationship. If you answer yes to any of the following questions, then you are most likely occupying the wrong role in this relationship:

1. Do you feel disloyal when acting differently than your parents? You know, that little voice inside you that says, "I would not approve of this" is not your conscience or Jiminy Cricket. That

meddling, controlling voice you perceive is your father's/mother's dominating personality invading your thoughts.

2. Are you afraid to express how you really feel or think in front of your parents? Some people are conflict-avoiders by nature. But when this gets to the point of completely hiding your emotions to please your parent, then you have fallen into the trap.

3. Are you more preoccupied about pleasing your parents than being yourself or making your friends happy? Are your priorities set correctly? In case you're in doubt, this is the correct order: Your happiness is first; can't make anyone happy before that. Were you expecting this to be second or third? Absolutely not. You are not responsible for pleasing anyone or making anyone's life more cheerful than yourself; the rest follows when it's appropriate for you to allocate your time and attention to your parents and friends.

Causes

I have a suspicion that my mother-in-law is in love or obsessed with my husband. As gross at it may sound, she treats Brett, my husband, as a surrogate spouse. The amount of emotional dependence she has on him is beyond words. Her marriage is awful, and she constantly complains about my father-in-law. She says things to Brett, such as, "I only stayed in this marriage for you and your sisters." To make matters even worse, she asked my husband to call her "Gorgeous" or "Beautiful," which is the way he usually refers to me. She was baffled when she found out I did not let him call her that and told him I was changing him. Of course, I changed him. I opened my husband's eyes and helped him see the twisted relationship he was in with her. Thank God Brett finally saw it and confronted her, telling her she leaned too much on him, and if there was something wrong in her marriage, she should fix it. She got offended and claimed she was perfectly happy with my father-in-law and that I had made him delusional.—NAMEAyra

> When our parents got divorced—which was twenty years ago—my younger brother was the only one of the four kids who hadn't gone to college. Since he suddenly became an "only child," my mother turned him into her surrogate husband right away. My brother spent the next two decades—his entire youth—anticipating my mother's desires and needs. Then he got married and had kids of his own, nonetheless bought a house next to her, in case she needed him. His attention is constantly divided between my demanding mother and his wife and children. Maggie

It happens a lot that when a parent gets divorced or loses their partner, they turn a child into the spouse they lost. When one member leaves, the other steps up and takes its place; it's their way of attempting to maintain a sense of balance (although if you asked me, it sounds pretty unbalanced).

Parents using their children to meet their emotional or financial needs think this arrangement works for everyone. They don't see the harm in their constant meddling because they think their children benefit from it. "I just want to help" is the common excuse. (Really, MIL? Do you want to help? Then bring me one of your yummy casseroles this Saturday, but don't criticize how I wash your grown-up son's sport socks.) In the mind of these parents, the exchange is a gain-gain situation: they get their needs covered, and their children feel useful.

Sometimes, it's not even the loss of a spouse that triggers the behavior. Many times, a father bears more control over a son because he has lost control over other parts of his life, such as his work. It's a natural reaction. The daddy loses control at his job and grabs it from wherever he can. Now, there are many ramifications to this type of behavior. Some parents remain involved in their daughter's finances, even though she is married and forty years old. And others will twist into eerie deviations such as, "I want my son to call me gorgeous, kiss me on the lips, and tell me I am the true love of his life." Double, triple yuck.

Making children play a role that doesn't belong to them is a heavy burden. In many cases, this behavior permeates to the children's relationships with other people and other areas of their lives. It can mess with their self-esteem or their ability to pursue their dreams.

Let's make a quick stop here, because we are now picturing parents as evil beings, and in all truthfulness, we do owe them a lot. From morning sickness to sleepless nights to endless sibling fights to saving money for college, most parents are heroes without a cape (Except for you, Aunt Tally; could someone tell the woman capes will never be in fashion? And that she is not a character from *GOT*?). So it is not only the father or the mother imposing this role over their children. Sometimes, the son or daughter voluntarily offers to fill the spot. For every case of a parent leaning excessively on a son, there is a son who wants to be perceived as the man of the house. "You are now the man of the house; you must take care of your mommy." Don't we hear this phrase often in the movies when Daddy is gone for whatever reason? And the boy proudly steps up. Little did he know it's one thing to be attentive to Mother's needs and another to be called at 2 a.m. two decades later because the cat is looking at her oddly.

The real cause behind it is as varied as Madonna's looks (I personally would've stayed at the "Hung Up" look; she was stunning). But in many cases, a narcissistic parent is to blame and trickier to spot. Because a narcissist is one of those people who seems to have it all: success, charm, good looks, popularity. If you relate to this situation, growing up with a narcissist parent, you probably could not get enough of them.

Narcissistic dads use people for their own good. They take advantage of their children and expect them to please him, no matter what.

Again, wipe off the image of an evil character; a narcissistic dad is charismatic. He loves being in the spotlight and receiving all sorts of attention. This dad brags about his prestige and brilliance, constantly exaggerating his achievements. He doesn't take criticism well and is incapable of feeling empathy for causes that he feels alien to him. There's another key characteristic: They ignore all personal boundaries and expect their children to fulfill their needs, running over their lives, relationships, and goals. They are experts at manipulating their children by withholding their love or blackmailing them so they get their way.

How Does This Behavior Affect a Child in Adulthood?

You can't teach an old dog new tricks; isn't that how the saying goes? Not to compare ourselves to a dog, but if a boy is trained to anticipate his father's needs when young, he will carry on into his adulthood. A daughter who turns into a surrogate wife to her father can neglect her marriage to put her father above her husband and learns to suppress her emotions and turn into a submissive wife.

A son who is used to being his dad's doormat can become pussy-whipped with every romantic partner or neglect all relationships, seeking for daddy's approval instead.

This type of behavior is especially harmful to that person's marriage. Like we said at the beginning, it's like the child is having an affair with the parent. This leaves the significant other in a crossroad. How much should she intervene? How much can he say or criticize his in-laws? Couples therapists say there are three sensitive subjects we should never tell our partners if we want to save our relationship: a) You have bad breath (Damn you, mouth-watering onion rings.). b) You are terrible in bed (Better rip that person's heart open instead). And c) Your parents are crazy, mean, stupid; you name it. Messing with your in-laws is one of the most difficult things you can do. (And by the way, I would add d) Your cooking is disgusting. Oh, really? For your information, I was told that salt and baking soda were interchangeable, you inconsiderate, ungrateful man.)

Anyways, if your spouse or partner is under this terrible spell (the emotional incest, not the terrible cooking part), your despair and frustration are completely understandable.

Daddy's Daddy/Surrogate Partner: How Does the Other Half Feel?

Decision-making dysfunction. All couples must be autonomous and have freedom to make their own decisions: where to live, how to manage their finances, how to raise kids, if they want kids, and so on. Having an overbearing in-law breathing down your neck, influencing your married life, can be enraging. An occasional suggestion is a good thing, but unwelcomed advice or orders can be the origin of bigger trouble. Now, background plays a big role here. Some people are just more used to ask for Dad's or Mom's advice, while others grew up learning to be independent. If you and your partner have different habits, problems can arise.

If this frustrates you, you must share your feelings with your spouse. And beware; asking for advice from your in-laws can open the door to more intrusions or even correcting you on decisions you make as a couple; slippery road, indeed. Sadly, with this type of parents, they may hold your marriage in high esteem, so you and your other half will have to fight hard to keep your independence.

Emotional apron strings. So your lovely hubby has been waiting for a job promotion for months; you've discussed it, dreamt about it, and cannot wait for it to happen. Then the day comes, and when you are ready to hear all the juicy details and celebrate, you find out your husband decided to call Daddy first. And his daddy decided to take him for dinner to celebrate; you are not invited this time. You are speechless, angry, and a little bit worried. Whenever a spouse gets his emotional needs met in his relationship with his father, there's an issue. While you get monosyllabic responses, his father gets the deep, soul-pouring conversations. While you are asked to save money, your mother-in-law receives a generous monthly allowance because "the poor thing is all alone, even though she has plenty of savings." While your husband is considerate, loving, and caring with you, he turns aloof when Dad is present. Any of these scenarios is inappropriate.

There has to be a limit; set some boundaries. Respect for each other is crucial. Setting priorities is the only way forward. You come first, his parents second. If he cannot understand this, then you have a problem. Same goes for women. Her daddy cannot dictate her life anymore, nor is he the "man of her life"; otherwise, why go to all that trouble, serving shrimp to eighty people, dressing up in that shocking tuxedo, and saying "I do" if she only wants to please Daddy?

Sense of betrayal. My friend Claire complains that every time she gets in a fight with her husband, he runs home to Mother to spill the details and ask for advice. This is not only embarrassing and disrespectful, it also damages Claire's relationship with her MIL. And there are no boundaries for what they talk about. She said that they fought a while ago about something he had said about her at a party. When they came home, he tried to initiate sex, but she asked him to stop because she felt hurt, and the discussion began. Two days passed, and they were having dinner with her in-laws, and her MIL kept hinting about the whole thing. She said things like, "I wasn't aware you were so sensitive, Claire." Or "Did you know that abstaining from having sex with your husband makes them prone to cheat?" When Claire realized she knew every single detail about her fight, she turned mad with rage, while her red-faced husband kept his mouth shut and focused on the canapés. Why would he tell her that? Not only it was sick, but they had reconciled already. Claire said the weird looks and awkward comments went on for a while, until she finally let it go. Parents are not referees of a marriage; they can't be objective.

For those under the spell, your loyalty is to your spouse. That's rule number one.

Life is filled with difficult choices. Most of the time, these decisions do not leave everyone 100 percent happy. Relationship with in-laws is the perfect example of it. It is hard to figure out what the best thing to do is. When in doubt, support and believe your spouse. Always. No matter what.

Your priority should be to protect your family against any harm. This includes your parents. Husbands and wives with a conflicted parent relationship must create a front and make clear from the beginning that their spouse comes first.

> Oh, gosh, his mother. A world of conflict. Since I met her, I had the impression she did not like me very much. I could live with that, as long as my husband supported me, which he didn't. My mother-in-law criticized me constantly and even compared me with my husband's ex-girlfriends: "Teresa would've never done that," or "Teresa used to love to shop with me," and the fighting began. Whenever I told my husband, he would say, "You are crazy; Mom would never say that!" So then I replied, "You don't believe me? You think I am lying about this?" And the arguments were never-ending. We got divorced. I still cannot believe she pushed us to this. All I wanted was for my husband to say, "Hey, Mom, this is my wife, so cool it." It never happened.

Conclusion

How to Deal with It

So how does this knot get untangled? Who gets to pull the strings?

The first thing you must do is accept responsibility for your actions. Yes, you have controlling, demanding, narcissistic parents, but no one is responsible for how to respond to them but you. You decide how much they dictate your life, how much they interfere in your relationships. How you respond to them is also in your hands. You can do this the adult way or get overly angry and make matters worse.

Do not obsess about making your father happy. You dad's job is done; you are all grown up and hopefully happy and healthy. Now you go on and be a decent human being, and if you decide to procreate, please bring up honorable, environmentally responsible, emotionally mature tiny persons. The thing is, you have to please yourself—yes, please have a double scoop of rocky road, even though you are keto now—not please your parents

Do accept you will not change them. Nope, not, zip, zero, nothing. You will not change your mother. Just as she cannot control you, you must never attempt to control her. She is who she is. Yes, you may change the way you respond to her demands, and hopefully, this will change how she behaves, but that's it.

Do be grateful for what they did for you. The sacrifices, the sweat, the tears they shed over you are proof of their love. Your parents are amazing and did what they thought best. Like all human beings, they are not flawless. As long as you accept that, you are on the road of healing.

Do resolve the past and forgive. Suddenly realizing that you have been your parent's doormat or surrogate spouse is not easy. It may trigger some unwanted feelings inside you, and that's understandable. But remember that forgiveness is not about who you are forgiving; it's about you and the process of healing an old wound. You are voluntarily letting go of bad memories and bitter moments to be happier.

Do set boundaries and distance yourself if nothing else works. Everyone deserves an opportunity to redeem themselves, and so having an open conversation about confronting your parents would be the number one step. Calmly and respectfully explain how their behavior, actions, and sayings have hurt you and the ones you love. Then set the rules for the future and work on your relationship. If there is no other solution, if they refuse to accept the guilt, if they become unreasonable, for your own sake, you must put some distance between you and them.

We only have one life to live; having someone putting their foot over our neck can make it miserable. Even if this is your father or mother, parents should not be seen as a ball and chain. There. I just set you free.

Chapter 4

PLAYERS

F un players or heartless players; which one do you prefer?
A player is a player. Play, have fun, amuse yourself. It's all laugh and glee until your feelings get hurt. Until the game is being played on you. Until someone plays you.

Now, when it comes to players, you have several types. In this section, we will focus on two: the fun player and the heartless player. Generally speaking, players are usually irresistible; they are attractive, beautiful, charming, sexy, flirtatious; the list goes on. We are drawn to them like bees to nectar.

Since I am all about fun, let's begin with fun players:

> I really feel like I am in high school again, but I am flummoxed. I've been dating this man for four months. Once the three-month milestone had been reached, and since he'd never discuss our relationship status, I asked him up front about our status. He said he wasn't "cut out" to be a boyfriend and wanted to be friends. I believe it. "In all honesty," I replied, "I wish I could also keep it casual," since I liked him so much, but I was ready for something serious. I wanted a committed relationship; I still do. So we stopped having sex. I put a clear boundary between us and inevitably began dating other people. Out of the blue, this man reaches out for me and wants to do very "relationship" stuff: spending the holidays with

me, popping up at my house with flowers, getting upset if I mention other men, etc. I have always been clear and direct, and I thought he was sincere as well. So what am I doing wrong? Should I go back with him to where we left? Will he ever commit? I am tired of the games.—Jean

Argh; I feel you, Jean. The endless circle of "I want you, but I'm scared to commit, but I don't want to lose you, but please stop pushing me." You find yourself more confused than when you tried to watch *Twelve Monkeys* or *Citizen Kane* (seriously, I need a podcast explaining both plots).

And you know what some men's lame excuse is: "We don't do it on purpose." Well, thanks, I feel so much relieved now that I wasted months, or even years, of my precious life on an ungrateful, childish person. Okay, let's say we agree. Let's say men do not purposely manipulate us to take some advantage; does that make them innocent? Heck, no. I mean, I had no intention of poisoning my neighbor's cat by offering him some peanut butter, but still, he ended up rushed to the vet's office, where they pump his guts out. Okay, so now I have to be considerate of other people's pet's allergies, preferences, and feelings? Yes, I do. And so do men.

Inconsistent and contradictory messages are to men what the moon diet is to women. Both say that's not their thing, and that is so cliché, it's laughable. But the truth is, we do it. They do it. All the time.

If complexity and strategy were inherent parts of the male personality, we wouldn't be having this discussion. They are not wired—I am talking specifically about fun players—to systematically destroy us. Most of the time, they are indeed confused and indecisive.

And why do we magnanimously decide to ignore this? Because players are fun. They are charming, easygoing, open-minded, and they give our lives the excitement, rush, and freedom we sometimes want.

Fun players are distinguishable from every other stereotype out there. It's the guy or girl who keeps you guessing. It's someone who won't return your messages and then pops up at your door with a fun weekend planned and a smile to die for. So, you would say, what's wrong with that? Well, same as a frosted flax seed coffee cake, once you scratch the yummy surface, the insides are quite disappointing. Because despite what you say, the majority of us do not want to be alone.

So the fair share of us will at one point of our lives settle or commit to a serious relationship that includes the object of our desire.

The real question is, is your man ready to settle? Is he a fun player?

Let's look at the most common signs that will help us determine commonalities of fun players:

- He says one thing but does another. Have you ever seen *He's Not That into You*? (I'm not saying it's a realistic movie; come on. Ben Affleck's character does not exist, but we'll get to that.) There is a quote from the film, where a guy tells this girl that if a man is genuinely interested in her, he will show it. Actions speak much louder than words. So you're probably getting mixed signals because either your guy sweet-talks you but acts inconsistently or he does stuff that makes you think he wants something more, but he says he doesn't.

- The conversation, and your relationship, revolves around sex. Oh, yes; fun players are fun for a reason. To be fair, most relationships begin this way. The undeniable chemistry you have with this person explodes like a rocket each time you are together. You are fire, and he is your match. Oh, come on; puns are fun. Yet, after a while, the "I-got-to-have-you-right-here-right-now" phase naturally dissipates, and you move on to a more intimate stage. Not with fun players. They get forever parked in the sex zone. Does your guy tell you you're hot instead of you look beautiful? Does he continually tease you with sexually charged questions? Sorry to break it, but most likely, he already has an expiration date on your relationship.

- Two of my friends who worked together began to date. I warned her about the risks of dating this coworker, a guy who was known for never getting serious, but she refused to see reality. The beginning of the fling was thrilling. Between the secrecy of their relationship and after the consummation of their passion, my friend was on a steady state of excitement. But heat tends to burn, and she finally sensed it. First of all, there was no conversation between them that did not involve sex; if she attempted to discuss serious subjects such as work matters, he would twist things, and they would end up in bed, or he'd walk away. Then, she asked for something more. She wanted him to go to a family gathering as her boyfriend. After six months of dating, giving each other presents, seeing each other daily, he said that they were just friends, and he was not ready for anything serious. If she wanted to, though, they could continue with their fling. My friend said she had to think about it; imagine her devastation when, after less than a week, he showed up at a party with a hot chick wrapped around his arm. That was the first time in my life I was not proud of saying, "I told you so."

- He does not introduce you to his friends or family. Have you heard of that term "the boyfriend [or girlfriend] you'd take to Mom"? That's what this is about. Especially when we talk about men. I am not saying that after two weeks of dating, you should be playing pinochle with your future mother-in-law while you discuss possible names for the grandkids. But if you've been dating this person for months, and you still don't know his family or his friends, you are dating a fun player who wants nothing to do with you in the future.

- He does not use the term "girlfriend" or "wife" when he talks about you. And I want to make this super clear: Just because you've married the guy, that doesn't mean this does not apply to you. It only means that somehow, he caved. But if he still shows any of these signs, you're in as much trouble as the next girl. My friend got married to one of those guys who say, "I do not believe in institutionalizing love. Marriage is another type of government oppression, and by the way, I only eat homemade vegan cottage cheese." What stung him to propose is still beyond my comprehension; maybe he saw a sign in one of those obscure poetry books he loves. Anyway, after ten years of marriage and a daughter, he still refuses to call her "my wife." I mean, they pay bills, they go to the supermarket, the daughter goes to school, they binge-watch Netflix on weekends, but he still sees himself as an uncatchable free soul. Oh, grow the freak up. She is your wife, you guys are married, and yes, you are about to get a middle-age paunch from all that homemade cheese you cook. Each time they celebrate their anniversary, he rambles on social media about how they are friends and partners, but he refuses to label what they have. All you have, pal, is an immature attitude and deep commitment issues.

- He is a master at the disappearing act. Everything is going well; you and your partner are having fun and getting along, but every now and then, he simply vanishes. Two, three, four days pass, and you start to wonder if he was abducted by aliens or had a heart attack. Then as unexpectedly as he disappeared, he shows up, all fresh, while you are left to wonder what the heck happened during his absence. And here's another trick: he not only vanishes every now and then, he coincidentally calls you to hang out in the after-hours. Girl, if your guy only calls you when the grocery store downstairs is closed, you do not have a committed relationship. You have a booty call.

- He tells you he has commitment issues. Surprisingly, fun players almost always tell the truth. Not regarding who are they are seeing, or what they are doing when you're not around, but regarding his posture regarding a potential relationship. Some guys are more subtle and simply begin to shake a poodle at the vet when you mention the words "commitment" or "relationship." If your guy is a bit more direct, he will let you know he does not plan to tie the knot any time soon. Those trite, stupid phrases you hate? "It is not you, it's me"; "I am currently trying to find myself"; "You deserve better than me"; "The timing is just not right"; or "I want to focus on my Stairmaster contest right now" (there is a world championship for this, so don't laugh), yup. They all fall into this category.

Have you ever felt you're always second-guessing and wondering where your relationship stands? Do you wish you would occupy a higher position on your partner's list of priorities? Well, dating a fun player feels exactly like that. And if you have to ask you these questions, then you probably are.

Now, let me tell you something about these people. They are not monsters. Okay, they are not exactly role models, either, but I see them more as immature Casanovas than scheming, diabolic womanizers. These people usually possess a charm, an irresistible quality that makes it impossible to reject.

Types of fun players:

- Anxious: "I do want a relationship someday, but I don't want you close to me."
- Scared: "I want to be committed, but I am too afraid to get hurt."
- Dismissive: "I don't want to be tied up, nor do I want someone clinging to me."

The therapists' offices are filled with people who are afraid of commitment. They may come from a dysfunctional family, experienced a traumatizing relationship, or watched too many episodes of the *Kardashians* and simply view committed relationships as phony and harmful. Whatever the reason, let me save you the suspense. Your man or woman will eventually commit.

Don't be jumping for joy yet. I didn't say he will commit to you.

You see, out of the three types I mentioned above, the first one can encompass the other two. To this day, I haven't met a single person who voluntarily is alone, who does not want to find someone. So, unfortunately, although fun players will put an end to their games eventually, it's unlikely they'll do it with you. You want to know why? Because he would've done it already. Let me tell you two different stories to clarify it.

Let's begin with Shanna, who swears she turned her untamable, fun player into a committed, devoted partner:

> From day one, I knew it. He was not an easy shot. He had never been in a committed relationship, nor did he want to. He referred to me as his "sort of girlfriend with no exclusivity or commitment." But with patience and dedication, I began a journey toward a trustworthy relationship. I put incredible amounts of effort into planning and operating an effective strategy. The number one rule was to never let my emotions control the situation. So I hid them. My frustration, despair, anger, sadness: I swallowed them. I also hid my fears and weaknesses. It took me fifty-two weeks to achieve it, spent in a roller coaster. While the beginning of our casual relationship

was a honeymoon—filled with hot dates, cooking together, enjoying day trips, etc.—he turned from casual to aloof. I had two options: let him go or become a love strategist. And I reached my goal.

Oh, for Pete's sake, Shanna. Really? From the two options that included being sane to becoming obsessed over an immature fellow, you chose the latter? You know what will happen, right? He will move on. I am not cruel or pessimistic, but love is not something that you plan coldly. This is a relationship that is supposed to be based on trust, enjoyment, affection, and other lovely things; this is not a monthly marketing plan. Strategies? You are wrong, girl.

And don't tell me just because Shanna or your cousin Zelda convinced their guys to be in a committed relationship, the whole scheming and manipulating approach works. It just means that they are the absolute rare exception, or their guys will eventually bail.

Okay, I am dating a fun player. What should I do?

You are not doomed. Just because you are involved with a fun player, that does not mean you are in for disappointment and hurt (unless you also watched Miss Bala, then you will hate yourself). Fun players are fun. And not all relationships have to end up with you in front of the altar, swearing, "I'll try" (sorry, an "I do"). So what's left? To manage your expectations.

Have you ever entered a restaurant and knew you weren't going to get the best meal of your life, but you're hungry anyways and decide to order? Dating a fun player is the same. The hamburger is greasy, the fries are too salty, but the overall experience is fun. And more important, it is transitory because you know that anytime you get tired of the greasy burger, you can walk across the street and eat delicious sushi at another restaurant.

So when you are enjoying your dates with your fun player, you also keep in mind that when the disappearing act gets old, or when you are ready for a serious relationship, you can always move on. If you take his blunders personally, or you expect more from his behavior, then maybe you are not cut out to be in such a situation. One thing you have to remember: you will not change him.

Fun players stop when they want. They become mature enough to realize that despite all the gibberish they say to girls, they do wish to settle in a meaningful relationship, be it a marriage or partnership. Let me finish with one last example, from Lauren:

> I met Ferd when I was in my early twenties, and we immediately hit it off. The dates were amazing, and I thought I had found the one. When months passed, I decided to have "the talk." He said he did not want anything serious, now or ever, and that he did not know how to be a boyfriend. He then said he loved how things were between us, and out of infatuation, I went along. We did all things boyfriends and girlfriends do; we went out, hung out with friends, saw each other during the holidays. But of course, days and weeks could pass without me knowing anything about him. I knew he was dating other girls, so one day, I cut him off. I told him we wanted different things, and with a broken heart, I said goodbye. Years passed; we dated different people in the meantime, and one day, he showed up again. He did not say anything different than the last time, but since he had sought me out after all that time, I thought he had changed. I thought I could convince him to change his behavior and fall in love with the idea of a committed relationship. That same damaging pattern happened a couple of more times. Then I met my husband, and I knew if I blew things with him to wait and see if the lone wolf finally turned into a knight in shining armor, I would end up alone. So I erased him from my life. Thanks to social media, and due to friends in common, I just learned he got married and has a kid! The uncatchable, the loner, the free spirit, the misunderstood, the maverick is now changing poopy diapers and burping babies at two in the morning. There's no such thing as a free spirit; he just needed to mature. And I was never his option to do so.

Finally, an insight to a retired fun player's theory, who believed it to be true till he matured one day:

To have women, you need two factors: time and money, so the possibility of having a woman can be measured like this: amount of money you have multiplied by the time you have to invest in her.

So, Women = TIME × MONEY

Time is MONEY (known fact, right?)

So, Women = MONEY × MONEY

Women = $Money^2$

Money is the root of all troubles, so

Money = $\sqrt{Trouble}$

We finally get the result:

Women = Trouble

Heartless Players

At the beginning of the section, I told you there were two different types of players: fun and heartless. While the first makes you lose your time and temper, the second ones can suck the life out of you and then peacefully move on to greener pastures.

Heartless players are those who take advantage of their partners—financially, socially, or otherwise—to advance in life, and then they enjoy the harvest with somebody else. This is beyond basic cheating; this includes deceit and being left with feeling empty.

Your friend has been agonizing about this guy; he is ripped, a guy who lives in the gym, and you can tell by his six-pack that he's always flashing his package. But of course, his little general is worthless. Meaning, it doesn't work. Either it is pumped by steroids or is just useless. That's the perfect description of this type of guy.

Let's start by listening to Kiki's outrageous story:

> I had been going out with my man for four dates. In the last
> one, he told me he was broke; I saw his confession as sweet.
> We began dating officially, and I was his cheerleader.
> He was going through a really rough stage; he needed
> rescuing, and I jumped on board. The problem was he
> kept losing jobs and therefore was continually out of cash;
> so I began to support him, as in paying for everything: my
> bills and his. Whenever he couldn't make rent, I would
> bail him out and also gave him the most supportive,
> loving pep talks. But being the only positive member of a
> relationship is difficult, and I began to question whether
> most of the drama in his life was self-created.
>
> Of course, I was not leaving him. I loved him. And I knew
> once he got over that ugly phase, we could finally begin a
> healthy, fun relationship. Slowly, things finally got better
> for him. He got a good-paying job, and the days where he
> asked me for money began spacing out. I thought, *This is
> it! My prayers have been answered.* But there was a catch.
> As soon as he began to do well, he became more motivated
> and ambitious, and then he accepted a promotion, which
> required him to spend time in a nearby city. Astonishingly,
> it became hard for me to get a hold of him. This was
> completely unusual, as I was usually his go-to person
> for everything. Then one day, he finally called. I sensed
> his seriousness and was already in my Wonder Woman
> costume, ready to save him, when he broke the news. He
> said he was doing fine, just very busy, and then he casually
> mentioned maybe it would be better if we went separate
> ways. After all I did for him, he left me. You want to know
> the catch? He's already seeing someone else.

Kiki asked herself what the heck happened. So you devote yourself
to polishing a guy, and then you are not the one who enjoys the fruit of

your hard work? Yes. That means you dated a bad player. You got used and abused.

So when you are in a relationship, a certain amount of synergy is expected, you know, the whole one plus one equals three. If you are not going to turn into a better version of yourself—smarter, happier, healthier—then why are you in a relationship? And nothing sounds more heroic to be the muse for your man to change, to be the one who inspires him to get a better job, to become thin, or to learn how to put his dirty socks in the damn basket. But there is a vast difference between building something with your man and building your man.

This is Regina's story:

> I met Regina, my friend, when we were both in college. She's always been physically attractive, and while her dream had always been to be married and have a family, men did not take her seriously. They saw her as a trophy; someone to show off, not someone to commit to. A few years ago, she thought she finally met her match, someone who liked her and admire her. But then, the boyfriend's influence became noticeable to all of us who loved her. While Regina has always been fit, she turned things up a notch and hired a personal trainer. She became obsessed, to the point of looking anorexic (I'll never know if she became sick or not). Friends and family became worried about her, but I knew she was only trying to please her boyfriend. She did not want to lose the only one who had finally committed. She became so detached from her older version of herself that we grew apart. I know the guy quit his job and depends entirely on her. I know he still has not proposed or anything close to it. And the worst part: I know my friend is not happy.

You know the famous phrase, "Behind every great man there is a woman." Yup, it's true, but it does not always work out for us women. Excuse me? And why do we have to be the ones supporting this man, helping him pursue his dreams? What about ours? Who is behind us?

Let's be fair. Society has changed. From the 1950s, when women were expected to look radiant, keep the kids quiet and clean, and have dinner ready by 5 p.m. so the tired husband could come home and finally relax, things have certainly changed. But something about that feeling still lingers here. The sentiment that we as women are the key for a man to become successful is quite unfair. But society expects that from you, and the same treatment is not required for men. Who asks a man to bend over so his woman can achieve her potential? Oh no; heaven can spare them from suffering because they demand a lady in the streets and a wild feline in the bedroom.

And while Kiki's example related to money issues, this is the truth for everything else. If you've been building your man, here's a mantra you must repeat to yourself daily: "I will not enjoy the fruits of my efforts."

This is Bea's story:

> I began dating Lucas when were both in law school, and he struggled with his grades constantly. Even from that moment, I became his savior. Neglecting my own work, I would dedicate endless nights with him, finishing papers and studying. He wanted to pursue a career in politics, which I thought laudable and inspiring. Now that I look back, I can see that our lives revolved around him: his problems, his aspirations, his desires. I would simply bend to accommodate his needs. Not long after college, he proposed, and we got married. His political career was not happening at all, so I had to take jobs that were miles apart from my area of interest so we could pay the bills, while he "worked the ladder." He went to lunches and took trips, getting to know people, while I spent my days in a job that I abhorred. I told myself my sacrifice would eventually pay off. Days passed, and he would come home, dragging his feet, complaining about how this guy was blocking him or that person was keeping him from getting a decent position. Some days, I would get tired of his whining and casually mention that maybe he had to pay his dues, start low, and then rise. He would flip off, we would have an argument, and I would end up apologizing.

The thing is, I loved him, and I truly believed in him. His stubbornness finally became effective, and he landed a respectable position in his political party; he was one of the campaign managers for one of the favorite candidates for an upcoming election. He was happy, but I was ecstatic.

He became busy, more and more each day. Sometimes, he would pull all-nighters. I told myself to be patient; he was finally launching his career. Then the little time he spent with us—we have three children—he was either looking at his phone or distant and indifferent. Not six months had gone by when he broke the news: he had met someone else, someone who also worked in the campaign, a young, bubbly blonde girl; I felt more haggard, sad, and outraged than ever in my life. Within a year, they were happily married. And two years after we split, they had twin girls. Now I look at his pictures on social media, where he portrays himself as a respectable, devoted family man with a promising career; he's still climbing and gaining recognition. Ironically, what happened to me happened to a couple of more wives. The slogan for the campaign had been "Get a new, improved life." But those morons still joke about it and say it was supposed to be "Get a new, improved wife."

If you've ever been through a divorce, you can relate to this. Especially if you devoted your time to building this man up, helping him getting more educated, richer, healthier, and so on. And I do mention healthier because I have at least a couple of acquaintances who were married to clinically obese men who found someone else after losing tons of weight. Why?

I am no psychologist, but the reason appears to be very simple. Bad players are leeches; unintentionally or not, they suck whatever they can from their partner and move on. Why not stay? Why the ingratitude? Because this new version of themselves, they feel, is incompatible with their old life, which, sadly, includes you. Their self-esteem improves, they get to know new people, and suddenly, a voice inside them whispers, "You deserve better. You can have better." And this entitlement leads to a breakup or a divorce.

In all truthfulness, the reality is, they can't cope with the fact they were something less than what they are today. They do not want to recognize who they were, so everything that reminds them of their previous life (before the new job, before their new education diploma, before Miss New Boobs) is repulsive to them. Unfair? Hell, yes. Preventable? Of course.

Why does being a woman mean "I'll cross the Sahara to save you." No, sir. Thank you, Brett, I hate the heat. I don't like the feeling of sand in my shoes. I ain't crossing no desert. So, Brett, I will love you from the comfort of my shade, sipping my Gatorade, while you hurry up and come to me. Be a good boy and hurry up, will you?

Years and years of brainwashing have really meddled with women's psyche. If you are in love, you are irrational, crazy, sacrificing; otherwise, you're just cold and emotionally unavailable. What happened to Kiki and Bea occurs every day, sadly. Devoted women give up the best years of their lives to build up their men, to help them achieve. For what? For a future that involves a divorce or a breakup, that leaves them devastated and hurt, while men move on faster than you can say Jack Robinson.

So if you have stuck with me so far, listen to this: Self-sacrifice is not worth it. We, as women, need to stop believing it is our job to unconditionally love a man. Unconditional love is a fake concept literature and movies have fabricated to convince us we should love someone even though they might suck on our necks and kill us at any moment (thank you for that, *Twilight*). We need to stop self-flagellating for wanting something more for our lives than being the woman behind the great man.

Let me clarify something here: There is absolutely nothing wrong with supporting your partner so can he achieve his dreams. Heck, if you're not in a supportive relationship, why bother then? But it must go both ways. If there's a great woman behind a successful man, then there should also be a great man behind you. Equally supportive, equally caring, equally loving.

Let's take a look at the ladies; they are similar to men, with a little tweaking:

"Tonight will be the night," my good friend Darren told me one random night. He had been dating his darling Isabella on and off, flirting with her over $250 bottles of wine. She would respond to his flirtation by keeping him on his toes and playing hard to get. But tonight was going to be different; he would show her how much she meant to him. Darren was ready to commit, and he sensed his Isabella would finally be his. Lovely, sweet Darren, all excited, went to the barber to sort out his look, got his suit dry-cleaned, and spent hours looking in the mirror, conversing with himself to get ready for his beautiful one Isabella. She looked stunning in her short black dress. It was going to be perfect, the date of his dreams, laughing and kissing over cocktails. Then, halfway through their romantic date, Isabella's face lit up as Steve showed up.

Isabella had mentioned Steve other times; he was her friend. When he said he'd be in town for the weekend, Isabella casually mentioned the restaurant she'd be with Darren. After an awkward dinner, Steve suggested going to a couple of hot parties. Darren was befuddled but reluctantly agreed to the plan. Suddenly, the most romantic day of his life turned into a weird frat party for adults. The best part? After tons of beer, Isabella went to spend the night with Steve. Darren was devastated, to say the least. What just happened?

You see, "player" is a moniker that is usually associated with men. Like it or not, it surely applies to women as well. Female players, just like dudes, are always going out with several suitors, grabbing their attention (and sometimes their wallets) until they finally go for one of them, or not.

Great conversationalists, impeccably well-dressed, usually physically attractive, and very flirty. Darren said to me, "She just presented herself in such a great way. It's like dating a character from a movie." They have all these funny stories to tell; they are sexy, beautiful, and captivating. Men who date them consider themselves lucky and smart. That's what keeps them going back. Secretly, they feel as fab like them when they are together.

So how do you spot a woman player? What are the signs? They are similar to the men's signs:

- They use men as placeholders. Okay, so you've been dating this Carrie Bradshaw type for a while; everything was going fine, but you notice her eye starts to wander. Maybe she picks a fight out of nowhere, and that behavior turns more frequent. Perhaps she doesn't even bother to discuss matters anymore. Her friends begin to withdraw from you, as if they know you are old news. Then, she avoids your texts and calls, and of course, sex is something you only see on late TV. Wake up. These are all hints of her wanting to end the relationship. At first glance, this is not precisely wrong, except they do it cruelly. If she were a decent person, she'd take you to your favorite café and let you go softly. If she's a genuine player, she won't even bother to face you. Or even worse, she'll keep dating you until she finds someone better.

- They emotionally manipulate men. What's the worst thing for a guy when dating a girl? Okay, aside from shopping. Okay, aside from picking up tampons at the store. Okay, aside from having to call her "my honey lambchop" in front of his coworkers. Yes, you guessed it: to see a woman cry. But these players use their emotional side to disarm men. You can see these displays in the form of childish tantrums or drama scenes worth of an Oscar.
- They are hot and cold. One minute, she is the sweetest girl you've ever met; the next, she makes Cruella de Ville look like a nun. This manipulation tactic is often used by players.
- You are always available for her, but she's not. She needs money, attention, a date; she's bored, and she calls you. And, of course, you answer in a heartbeat. This is the girl of your dreams. But God forbid you need something from her, and suddenly, she is too busy or has important things to do, but she is so sorry. Players are also known for cancelling plans at the last minute. Even if you purchased those concert tickets a month ago and went over your budget because she wanted good seats, she won't hesitate to call it off if it suits her plans.

When a sexy girl acts interested in you, it's exciting. You feel good about yourself because you realize you are capable of attracting a cool, gorgeous woman. When her interest fades, meaning when she's done using you, the great sensation turns bitter.

Conclusion

Fun player, bad player. One messes with your head, the other one messes with your heart and entire life.

Surprisingly, some of us know our other half is a player and yet act like we do not mind being in the queue to get some attention whilst he shags half the block, your friends included. If you are okay with this on-and-off relationship, who are we to judge? If not, then being in denial is not the ultimate solution, as resentment follows next.

But there is no need for us to learn about these outcomes the hard way. All we have to do is be honest with ourselves.

If you're dating a fun player, be aware you will not be the one he settles with; if you are dating a heartless player, you will not be the one he spends the rest f his life with.

There is a saying in some cultures that claims you should marry your equal, and I totally support the idea. To marry someone less than you is to lower your standards and renounce a great future. You may sacrifice yourself to help unleash his potential. Just to realize he will be a better partner in his new relationship.

Don't do it. Marry someone at your level, or even better, marry someone at a higher level than you. Make him aid you in achieving your dreams for a change. I know you have devoured romantic movies and thought, *I would do anything for love too,* but don't fall for the trap.

Please let me say it loud and clear: There is nothing wrong with pampering your man, with helping him, especially during hardship. But there's a gap between an ambitious man with a plan and a wishful, life-sucking leech. The first is worth sacrificing for; the second is not.

Chapter 5

NARCISSIST

Y ou probably know what the word *narcissist* means. It describes someone who continually brags about his bank account and admires his own reflection in a puddle, right? Not quite. It's deeper than that. A narcissist is a self-centered person who makes everyone else around him miserable and still expects them to apologize to him. A narcissist is a person who trips over your feelings and emotions; once he gets up, he says, "I am okay; I just brushed that crap off me."

You may be laughing right now, but this is a serious matter. I mean dead serious, unlike that time you thought you were in a serious relationship just because Gary accidentally texted you the hearted-eyes emoji when he actually wanted to send you the poop emoji. (Oh, Gary, grow the fuck up.) Anyway, narcissism can lead to severe problems in a relationship, from lowering someone's self-esteem to verbal, physical, and sexual abuse. Psychologists and psychiatrists seem to agree on narcissism being part of the sociopath spectrum.

If you are in a relationship with a narcissist, it can be challenging to explain what's going on. For instance, some people claim to feel lonely in a relationship, yet they don't know why. You may think you always say or do the wrong thing, and this causes your partner to get angry. Although you have good intentions, you seem to set him or her continuously off.

In fact, it is not uncommon to hear people compare being involved with a narcissistic to living in a cult; it's like the whole Branch Davidians ordeal, minus the repulsive handsomeness of David Koresh, the guns, and prophecies. You get my drift. To make matters worse, living in a sect at least gives you a sense of belonging and companionship. Of course, that lasts until a fellow cult member shoots you. Anyway …

There is a lot to dig in, regarding narcissistic behavior. Let's start with a more formal definition, for the sake of keeping the ritual.

Narcissism is a mental condition (don't try to blame it on hormones this time) in which people have an enhanced sense of entitlement and self-importance; they demand excessive attention to their needs and desires, but they completely lack empathy for others. Their key point? Troubled, conflicted, turbulent personal relationships.

A narcissist taints every area of his life with his hurtful, confusing, and vicious behavior; his work, finances, family, and romantic partners are daily targets.

Signs

You may say, "Sure, but that definition can apply to many things." It's like when you are watching TV, and an advertisement for a pill pops up. The man asks, "Have you been experiencing nausea, extreme tiredness, frustration, sleep deprivation, and mood swings? Then you are suffering from a severe ailment. Domperidone can help you feel great again." I mean, come on, those are the same exact symptoms of parenthood. I'm sure that by popping two Domperidone (isn't that the most excellent name for a medicine, ever?) daily, my parenting symptoms will go away, right?

That's why we need more information and signs. Here are the most common indications of narcissistic behavior:

- They have an exaggerated sense of self-importance. By the way, narcissists and social media are a dangerous mix. These people feed on stupid things such as how many likes did they get for that idiotic photo of them climbing a little hill on their vacation (especially when accompanied with hashtags such as #lifegoals or #adulting. Please roll your eyes with me).

Jayde recalls one morning in which her husband Pete greeted her; she did not hear him asking her how she slept. Jayde says, "He flew into a rage, screaming at me for not greeting him back and for not staying in bed a few minutes to cuddle. I had never experienced such drama. He continued to yell at me, telling me how disrespectful I was. I apologized like a million times. He shook his head and said I would never find anyone else to put up with me."

- They require constant and excessive admiration. Sort of stepping on the last point, but in this case, they request their loved ones to praise them verbally. "Why didn't you compliment my new haircut, honey?" "Because I already told you ten minutes ago, it looks awesome." "Oh, so you fulfilled your daily quota for love demonstrations today?" "Cindy, that's not what I meant." "Bite me, Jack!"
- They exaggerate achievements and talents. "So what's your current profession?" "I'm exploring my painting abilities, mostly abstract. I consider myself this generation's Pollock." Friend turns in disbelief. "Oh please, Simon, you took one lousy online course of painting by numbers, and suddenly you are an artist?" Narcissists think everything they do is sensational; mainly because they believe the sun shines from their behinds.
- They monopolize conversations; they criticize and belittle those who do not agree with them.
- They take advantage of others. They expect favors done for them when they are unwilling to reciprocate.
- They are unable to acknowledge, listen to, or pay attention to the needs and feelings of other people.
- They must have the best of everything. If they are married, they must have the best car, the better side of the bed, the last piece of cheesecake, you arrogant, pretentious individual.

Causes

Surprise, surprise: Science does not know what exactly causes this personality disorder. Don't these people (doctors, scientists, and psychiatrists) spend decades studying humans, and still they don't know? Oh, but I bet if you ask someone on the street to explain her partner's astral chart, she will come up with several reasons why he is such a shitty, selfish person. "His mummy carried him too much during an eclipse. He was a slave in his past life, so his spirit swore revenge." Yeah, right. I will stick to the traditional approach. No known cause.

In defense of health professionals, this syndrome, despite being common, is quite complicated. But yes, these factors make people prone to become a narcissist:

- Upbringing. Do you always tell your daughter she is better than the rest of her peers? Do you call your son "my king"? Do you say to your children they are perfect? Well, I am not saying you are raising egotistical, self-absorbed little people; but this type of behavior does not help.
- Genetics. I told you hormones played no role in this one, didn't I? But genetics is the common answer when people don't have the slightest idea of what to put the blame on. "Why am I overweight? Oh, it's genetics" "Why can't I dance the mambo like my cousin Wilma? Mmm, I guess because of genetics." "Why does my partner insist on eating beans with ketchup? You know why? Genetics."

Keep in mind that while children may exhibit traits of narcissism, that doesn't mean they will become sociopaths when they grow up. In fact, there is no better example of narcissistic behavior than a newborn. Think about it. They only care about their needs. They absolutely have no empathy for their sleep-deprived, angry, tired parents; they demand attention and will throw a tantrum if their desires are not fulfilled. Okay, okay, those chubby, chunky legs are worth it; I admit it. My point is, you can never tell if a person is truly a narcissist until adulthood.

Cause of the Cause

So, going 100 percent against what they seek, let's remove some of the spotlight from them and focus on the victims. This is how I see it: You've got a selfish, self-absorbed, abusive person. What happens if no one pays attention to him? What happens if he has no one around to enable his hurtful behavior, to stand and listen to his complaints and attacks? In other words, what happens if no one takes up his shit? What was first, the egg or the chicken? (I always like this one; makes you really wonder, right?) Because if we leave all narcissistic people alone, maybe ship them off to an island where they would fight to get a seagull's attention, where does that leave our victims?

Are narcissistic people born that way? Or do we enable them?

The first thing to decipher is whether you are romantically involved with an narcissist. If you are, trust me; you are not alone.

Signs You Are Dating a Narcissist

We've covered their part. How does a narcissist look from outside? We know it. But we are not outsiders, are we? We are so profoundly in the mess that retrieving a missing sailboat from the Bermuda Triangle would be less complicated than removing ourselves from a tormented relationship with a narcissist. Mostly because we fail to see it. Don't worry; I've got your back. Let's analyze your relationship (enough about them) and see what we find, shall we?

- He was too charming, at first.

Don met Patty online. After chatting for several days, they decided to meet at a popular restaurant for their first date. Don seemed like a gentleman and was incredibly good-looking. After some small talk, he turned the conversation into a more intimate one. He began asking Patty about her past life, even asking such things as how many sexual partners she'd had so far. Hinting did not work for Patty, so she said bluntly, "Can we please change the subject? Your questions are turning too personal, and frankly, I feel uncomfortable."

To her surprise, Don seemed upset and even angry; he said, "I am just trying to get to know you better."

After dinner was over, Patty said they should just be friends, as she wasn't interested in a romantic relationship with him. Again, Don showed signs of anger, and they both parted ways. Next week, Patty began receiving tons of messages, flowers, and gifts from Don, asking for a second chance. She didn't know what to do. He was super hot, and she decided that a second chance was not a bad idea.

Is this a modern fairy tale? Not entirely. Actually, the fact that your significant other relentlessly pursued you at the beginning (texted constantly, unexpectedly showed up at your job, showered you with gifts) is quite common among narcissists. There's a totally awesome term to describe it: love bombing. Here's how their twisted mind works: He meets someone; that someone (you) detects something odd or unpleasant about him and rejects the possibility of a relationship. Then, instead of accepting your decision, he vehemently tries to conquer you. Not because he is genuinely interested, but because he feels entitled to you. It is a matter of winning; he is not interested in getting to know you. He will never allow someone else to dismiss him; he has to be the one who dumps you.

Nonetheless, people—especially ladies—are suckers for romance. Damn you, Hollywood. And damn you, Mr. Darcy. We see this wooing as flattering and fall immediately for the trap. I am not blaming you, they are indeed, truly, charming. So, a piece of advice here: if he or she is coming too keen on you, despite your rejections, be wary.

- He hogs the conversation.

Glendy got home after a job interview. She couldn't wait to share the news with Trent, her dear hubby; this position was something she had dreamed about for months, if not years. And she finally had it. When she got home, Trent barely greeting her and said, "I am glad you came home; something happened at work."

Glendy was surprised he did not ask her about the interview but said, "Okay, but let me first tell you ..."

Trent, ignoring her, began to ramble on about how he had pitched an amazing idea to his boss, who compared his work to Nike's brilliant "Just do it" tagline, while Glendy patiently waited for her turn. After an hour of nonstop talking, he then proceeded to recall his achievements as a college student and claimed he could've chosen to work with Steve Jobs. By the time he was done, Glendy was exhausted. As Trent stood up and walked toward their room, he asked, "What did you want to tell me, anyway?"

A weak light crossed Glendy's eyes; he was finally interested. She said triumphantly, "I got the job."

Trent frowned and replied, "I thought the interview was next week."

Sound familiar? Do you find yourself continually struggling to have a voice in your relationship? How much of the conversation between you and your partner is about him? That's a thinker, right?

- He picks on you, all the time.

Teasing your partner here and there is not harmful; in fact, it adds spice to the relationship. Now, take your mind off dirty thoughts here; not that kind of teasing. I mean making innocent jokes. For instance, my husband does not like me to remind him of his house chores, as it makes him feel I am bossing him around. So every time I ask him to do something, such as taking out the trash, he replies, "Yes, Mummy." To which I reply, "I am sorry, babe. I know you will eventually do all those things. No need for me to remind you every six months to hang that mirror, right?" That sort of thing; it sounds funnier in person. My point is, joking and mocking each other is entirely innocent and fun. Of course, you are not going to make fun of things he is insecure about, right? For instance, I would never talk about my hubby's goofy walk or the way he involuntarily spits when he is talks excitedly about something. That would hurt him.

A narcissist partner will do exactly that. Hurt you, with spiteful, wounding comments.

I have a really hot friend. I mean, she has a Baywatch body. Her ex-boyfriend, by comparison, was a slob, tall, ungracious man with a flabby paunch and a ridiculous hairdo. I'm not judging, just stating the facts. One day, they went shopping at the mall, and they went to Abercrombie and Fitch. You know the store? It's where all the fit, beautiful, tan, people work. Well, first of all, my friend's guy started to flirt shamelessly with the cashier, asking questions, laughing at her jokes, all in front of my friend.

In my opinion, the conversation between a cashier and a customer should be reduced to three sentences: "Good afternoon." "Cash or credit?" and "Thank you for shopping with us." Anything else is extra. No need for it. Even asking, "Did you find everything you were looking for?" seems kind of redundant, doesn't it? You wouldn't be paying if you didn't find an item; what is she going to do? Pop it magically out of her firm chest?

Anyway, going back to my friend. Once they left the store, the guy suddenly turned to her and said, "Did you see those boobs and those tempting full lips? And the tiny waist. Oh my! [His eyes filled with lust.] I mean, you are never ever going to look like one of those girls, right?"

I feel like vomiting every time I remember all the mean things he said to her, from making stupid comments about her body to mocking her taste in books (he was a fool who wouldn't read the back of the cereal box) to ridiculing how much money she had. He even mocked her for not having as many friends on social media as he had. I told you, Instagram and narcissism is a lethal combo. And you know why he did all those things? Because narcissists want you to know you are no better than they. In fact, nobody is.

- He lacks empathy.

Empathy is the ability to feel how another person is feeling. Well, the lack of it is one of the hallmarks of narcissism. Let me tell you this story:

Antonia had been married to Rupert for over a decade. She had endured his awful behavior toward her for the sake of the marriage and for the children. Nothing he did to her seemed to make an impact; he would embarrass her, belittle her, and withhold sex whenever he wanted; of course, he had multiple affairs. Nonetheless, she fought fiercely for her marriage. Despite the absence of sex, intimacy, and overall love, she stuck with it. Then, tragically, she got cancer. Don't think for a minute this life-changing event turned his heart around. He's a real douche. Anyway, one day, after a terrible chemo session, they were driving back to their house when she let a soft moan out. She was in pain and had terrible nausea. Well, this son of a bell stopped the car and began yelling at her and telling her she was overreacting. Bewildered, she said she could not help feeling that way, so he showed her his fist and threatened her to give her something to cry about.

This guy's wife, a loving, devoted person, was going through one of the most terrible things a human being can endure. And still, there was no dash of empathy, compassion, or love in him.

His ability to mistreat her was equal to her ability to endure it. Why would a beautiful, successful, smart woman undergo such treatment? Did she somehow set him off? What pulled the trigger? We'll go back to that one in a second.

- He thinks he is right about everything. It is impossible to have a civilized discussion with him.

Cathy was doing the dishes after dinner. She heard her dog, who was sick, gagging and knew projectile vomiting was next. Catty had two choices: finish the dishes or clean up the mess she knew was waiting for her in the TV room. Cathy chose wrong.

Catty's husband, who was comfortably watching TV, saw the dog throw up. He expected his wife to stop whatever she was doing and clean the carpet. When she didn't, he completely lost it. He ran to the kitchen and screamed at her for being an idiot. Catty said he didn't speak to her for a couple of days, although she kept asking what was wrong. She finally gave up and apologized, numerous times. Then he stopped the silent treatment.

Fighting with a narcissist can be impossible. They don't know how to debate, compromise, yield, apologize, acknowledge, or agree. They are always right, even when they are not. They are complete morons. They will not even recognize a disagreement; they just view it as an opportunity for them to teach you some truth. A narcissistic partner cannot hear you and refuses to understand you or take responsibility for any problem.

Being in a relationship is all about negotiating. "Okay, I will put the kids to sleep if you rub my feet for an hour."

"I will pay for gas this month if you buy me that new computer I desperately want."

"Okay, I will wear that black thingie in bed if you tell me I look better than Scarlett Johansson." That sort of thing. In fact, when you get married, instead of exchanging vows, the priest, judge, or minister should give the couple a quick lesson on statistics: "Dearly beloved, we are gathered here to teach this couple of oblivious lovers how to add 50 percent and 50 percent. Also to give them some pointers on the theory of supply and demand."

Well, narcissists obviously skipped that lesson. Because aside from being unwilling to understand you, they will never, ever admit when they are wrong. If your significant other forgets to call when he was supposed to, shows up late for a dinner reservation, changes your plans at the last minute, leaves you stranded, or does anything that causes you discomfort or pain, he will never apologize for it.

Explosive fights are wrong, but they convince their partners that they are being drama queens. They have no trouble whatsoever twisting your actions or phrases to make you feel guilty. You know what's even worse? They will find a way to make it look like it was your fault, and you will end up apologizing for it.

Tanya was a gorgeous, stunning, narcissist. She and Alex had been dating for a few weeks. After a romantic dinner, they decided to take a tranquil walk through downtown and happened to pass a jewelry store. Tanya stopped at the window, admiring everything they had on display, and commented on how lovely everything looked. Since the store was still open, she suggested they go inside and take a look.

Alex felt a bit uncomfortable but didn't want to disappoint her, so they went inside. Tanya went straight to a showcase filled with bracelets. She tried a couple of them on, continually exclaiming how much she liked them and asking Alex for his opinion. She narrowed her choices down to two, saying, "You pick one, Alex."

He felt trapped; he had never intended to buy Tanya such an expensive gift, but since he said he liked one better than the other, he was cornered. He had to buy it for her. They walked out of the store, Tanya pleased, and Alex was feeling miserable, angry, and frustrated. Later, she sent a couple of messages thanking him for such an expensive present; Alex was somewhat cold in his answers. She abruptly became angry and sent a very long message, rambling about his aloofness and calling him "cheap and heartless." One day passed, and Alex called her to apologize. After some begging on his side, they made up. To this day, Alex does not understand what the heck he did wrong."

- He gaslights you. Basically you feel anything you do or say is wrong and then you get very aggravated to a point you look like a lunatic.

Again, let's turn the spotlight to you, the suffering, struggling victim. How do you feel about it? This is what narcissists do to their victims:

- You often think you are overreacting or blowing things out of proportion.
- You feel like everything you do is wrong.
- You automatically think everything is your fault.
- You apologize way too often.
- You make excuses for your partner's behavior.
- You feel anxious and not confident.
- You no longer feel like the person you used to be.

This last one is quite terrifying but true. When we think about victims of abuse, we visualize a feeble, insecure woman, huddled in a corner. Then you see yourself, at least the old version of you. You were confident, assertive, successful, smart, and beautiful. How could this happen to you?

This is like which came first, the egg or the chicken? You were a perfect, round, fresh egg. And not far away, there was a chicken. He was already a chicken; no pun intended, but yeah. He was a coward before he met you. After some time, he met you. And it worked perfectly for him. He now can fulfill his role by hatching you (for the umpteenth time, no pun intended). And the product is an awful, abusive relationship.

The thing is, you were attracted to him. The question you may ask yourself is, why? Why was I lured to this person? Here are some possible answers:

1. Lust makes us blind. And sexual attraction isn't always about behavior or communication. Heck, sometimes it doesn't have to do with love. Yes, I know, love is the best aphrodisiac, but at the very beginning, it's a purely animal thing. Better said, a chemical reaction. And that spark, that incredible connection, overcomes our judgment, and we overlook the obvious. The beast behind the beauty.
2. Seduction. Even if he is not a terrific lover, or even before you have the chance to prove it, there is seduction. Narcissists are skilled manipulators; they are charming, not just in the sexual aspect, but

at the beginning, they lure you with flattery and persistence. It is hard to ignore someone who seems caring and devoted.

3. Idealization. Quite often, narcissists are good-looking, powerful, rich, talented, and accomplished. It is quite natural for you to idealize because you want to partake in the benefits of his traits. Admiration is natural; you see someone bold and secure, and you stare in awe.

4. Codependency or low self-esteem. People with low self-esteem are naturally attracted to narcissists. It's their yin to their yang. If you feel you are not entitled to love and respect, you will be enticed by a guy who thinks the opposite. Let's be very careful about this point. Misconceptions abound. Don't believe that someone who is good-looking or accomplished cannot have low self-esteem. Just look at celebrities. Jennifer Lopez has publicly disclosed her struggles with insecurity, and Reese Witherspoon confessed she was a victim of domestic violence (one of them has an Oscar, and the other has a tooshie that deserves an Oscar). So low self-esteem has more to do with personal issues, childhood trauma, and other things than with external appearances or talent.

He throws a large stone at you. It cuts you and hurts you. Your codependency makes you forgive him instantly. A couple of weeks pass by, and you accidentally throw a rock at him. It barely makes a mark on him, but he is outraged, to say the least. He shows you the tiny pink mark on his skin and yells at you or else gives you the silent treatment. How could you do such a thing? It doesn't matter that he did it first and on purpose. If he ever forgives you, he will bring back this episode to make you feel guilty and ashamed.

Break It or Mend It?

You cannot change a narcissist. You cannot even make them happy by changing your desires or personality. It doesn't work that way. They will never be empathetic, and you will always feel empty and lonely. Not to mention physical damage or verbal abuse can permanently hurt you as a result. Nothing is ever enough for them, because they see themselves as perfect. The only thing you can do is cut ties. No explanation, no second chance.

There is no fix, no solution, no magic formula. Unless that person is willing to go to therapy for years, and you are ready to wait and help, your relationship is destined to end. Here are a few things that will prepare you for the imminent breakup:

- Ask your friends and family for support.
- Remind yourself regularly that you deserve better. If necessary, think of all the things he did or said to you that hurt you.
- Go to therapy yourself.

When I say no second chances, I mean it. I am a firm believer in reconciliations. I believe that two people who love each other and have gone through a difficult patch can mend their relationship. In my opinion, this is not the case.

Narcissists panic when they see the red flag, the thing they never think will happen: you dumping them. You becoming independent. That will set him off. He will contact you and harass you until you take more drastic measures. Or until you yield to his pursuing.

Remember Rupert and Antonia, my friend with cancer? After that episode after chemo, she saw the light. It took two malignant carcinomas and five chemotherapy sessions for her to see it, to see eight years of abuse, of him embarrassing, downgrading, and neglecting her. The endless fights in which she apologized. The countless nights in which she longed for intimacy, or even a cuddle, but got the cold shoulder instead. Why? I keep asking myself.

Why does it take a life-changing occurrence for us to realize it? The only thing I can think of is because then, we realize how finite our existence is. Have you seen those workaholics who neglect their relationships and devote themselves entirely to work? Then one Tuesday afternoon, their doctor tells them they have six months to live. What happens to them? They quit their job, grab their families, take a quick trip to Venice (they had always dreamed of going), and finally take their wives in a gondola, where they recite a poem, and then get matching tattoos that say "Vida Loca."

Something similar happened to my friend. She saw her life flash before her eyes and asked herself, Is this all I am going to experience? Is there more life out there? Am I missing out on something?

> Sammy's husband Clark ran the house; he meant well, okay? Clark picked out Sammy's clothes, made makeup suggestions, and peered over her shoulder when she was writing the grocery list or when she was texting a friend. Clark also made sure to go through Sammy's phone. After all, he just wanted to enjoy the utmost intimacy with her. When Clark began traveling away from home, he installed CCTV cameras all around the house, just to check on her and make sure she was all right. After their relationship was finally over, Sammy realized she hadn't made a decision for herself in years. She needed to relearn everything, beginning by being herself again.

Conclusion

You are entitled to your own emotions, feelings, and thoughts. You deserve love, respect, and a reciprocating relationship. You need to understand that your ego was bruised, and it will take some time to recover. But acknowledging the problem is always the first step in the path of happiness.

After dating or being married to a narcissist, you often feel you were not treated like a human being, but as an object that was utilized whenever it was necessary.

Don't wait until it's too late, until your chances for real happiness have come and gone. Act now; do something for yourself today. Tomorrow may be too late.

As for those selfish, egomaniac, abusive individuals? Don't feel bad about them. They are not entirely useless; they serve perfectly as bad examples.

Chapter 6

AN UNFAITHFUL WOMAN'S POINT OF VIEW

For decades, women have been trying to prove to men that they're no different from them. They can run a country, they can lift weights, and they can grow a moustache (sorry, cousin Ellie). The point is, they are right. Try as I might, I cannot think of an action that only men can do. But that doesn't make us the same. In fact, we remain as different as ever.

We may perform the same actions. However, we go about it differently. We can fix a car—but we read the instructions first. We, too, bring work home—and at the same time, we feed a toddler, fold laundry, fix a faucet, and wash a unicorn. We also ask a friend for advice—after giving her a one-hour explanation with sounds and props. And we also cheat. But we do it differently.

Women violate their wedding vows for different reasons, during unusual circumstances, and with wholly different outcomes. Before taking a dip into these differences, let's examine the cheating disorders.

Just the sound of it makes you feel wrong: "cheating." You pronounce it and already hear a slap somewhere. No matter when or how, someone will get smacked. Modern society tells us cheating is wrong and immoral, especially for women.

Remember, for too damn long, we chicks were not allowed to express our sexual desires. Heaven forbid that we dared to speak about sex publicly. Big no-no. Locker-room talk was reserved for men. Women were expected to be loyal and submissive to our men. Not so long ago, women were taking courses in school on how to be a good wife, whereas guys were becoming engineers, doctors, and such. Meanwhile, mothers were having a hard time learning how to clean single-malt stains out of a white shirt. If things had been the other way around, I wonder whether the world would be as messed up. But that's a different subject.

Men cheat more than women. No, I am not fabricating this. This conclusion has been reached by many reputable sociological studies. The most common figure cited is around 70 percent (whereas 40 percent of women do). Out of ten guys, seven are unfaithful. Before feeling all self-righteous about it, four out of ten women cheat too. Perhaps I shouldn't sound as cheerful; the ultimate goal for me personally is monogamy.

And why, you may ask, there is such a difference? Is it because it's not in our nature? Is it because we don't have the same sex drive as men? Is it because we lack opportunities? Drum roll, please—none of the above is the answer. Fewer women cheat because we are conditioned by social norms to behave a certain way.

In the past, things were a bit different. Our loyalty, if you want to call it that, was enforced by the fact that most of us stayed at home. You may have heard the expression "opportunity makes the thief," which can be applied to material things. You don't leave your car keys unattended in a dangerous neighbourhood. In relationships, it would go like this: You don't leave your wife—with whom you haven't been intimate for two years—alone with the hot new coworker during the Christmas party, while she is drunk and wearing a dress so sheer you can see her thoughts. I am not saying that cheating, in this case, wouldn't be wrong. But come on. Can you really blame this woman? And still, we don't do it as often as men do. We have been sensitized to social pressure since forever.

But going back to my point. In the past, women did not cheat, for the simple reason that they lacked opportunity. Even if they were trapped in a miserable relationship, they were stuck at home, looking after a bunch of children. Where was this woman supposed to meet a partner to have a torrid love affair? You've heard the jokes about the milkman, haven't you? Well, there you go. The desire has always been there; the modern factor is the opportunity.

Women's liberation added two dramatic changes to this situation: First, many more women work outside the household. Women have more free time, more independence, more people they get to know. Ergo, more chances to meet someone else. The second change is women's attitude toward their sexuality. Sex is not about pleasing a man; the act should be enjoyable for both. Women have the right to choose when, where, and how much sex to have. (Same goes for men, to be 100 percent fair.)

Chicks are also more prone to experiment, which can be done with a steady partner. In fact, the best sex is achieved when two people are truly connected, when they share a bond that goes beyond physicality. If you add some spice to it, then you have the best shag in the world. And let's admit it: The movies lie to us blatantly. Here you have two strangers who get together for one steamy night, and everything goes perfectly. The guy is gentle, sexy, and not at all selfish. The woman reaches the stars at the end. In reality, he has coffee breath, and she really hates the way he tickles her cheeks. Chemistry is not instant or automatic. It takes work, people.

Now let's throw something into the mix, something no one saw coming: smartphones and social media. There you go. Now your opportunities to cheat are endless. You have flirting, breaking up, and sexual intercourse with the convenience of a single swipe on Tinder. The area turns as gray as Christian. Is sending a kissing emoji considered cheating? Is exchanging naughty pictures crossing the line?

Psychologists agree that women are more bothered by these lesser transgressions than men are. For men, basically, unless another guy sees you naked, you're fine. Are they really fine? Or is this acceptance a way for them to justify their own behavior? After all, one can only send so many naughty pictures before asking that other person out. And those kissing emojis have an intention—to turn them into real kisses, right?

Generally speaking, men and women have different reasons for sneaking around. Guys usually cheat because the opportunity is right there, though of course I am generalizing. Women, on the other hand, do it because they feel there's something fundamentally wrong in their relationship. A man sees his lover as inferior to his wife, as a hobby. A woman sees her lover a superior being, someone who will eventually replace her current partner.

Couples therapists say that the vast majority of unfaithful women have first gone through a process of frustration. They feel underestimated, neglected, and ultimately unhappy. I am not saying a guy cannot feel this way. But the difference is that more women are prone to express this disappointment verbally, as one last cry for help. Most women want to save their relationship. If nothing else works, they will cheat.

> After constantly telling my husband how unhappy and lonely I had been for years, he chose to ignore me, and he continued to take business trips for months at a time. I eventually moved on and found someone else. That someone else fulfils my needs at the time. More importantly, that affair gave me the courage to confront him and ask him for a divorce. I was done.—Anna

The funny thing is, most of this process occurs subconsciously, meaning that it is not something a woman plans. We plan Christmas shopping, our weekends away, and what to tell our bosses when we are hung over and miss a meeting. But we don't always plan infidelity. It is only after the fling has started, or even when it has ended, that the girl realizes why she did it: She was trying to fill the void inside her.

There's even a riskier approach. We are strategic creatures and not at all as straightforward as guys are. Some women cheat to prove a point, to appear more desirable in the eyes of their husbands, to force them to appreciate them. This is a hazardous business; your guy may never forgive you, or worse, he may not even care. So whatever the reason for cheating, it is not the way to go. I'm not advising you to be unfaithful, under any circumstances. But let's say you are on a keto diet, and you can't stand it. You *must* cheat. You crave carbs like nothing else in your life. Okay, go ahead. But for Pete's sake, don't do it with a Twinkie. Cheat for the right reasons, like a real Mexican taco or a big slice of pavlova.

The History and Biology of Cheating

> You want to know why I cheated on my husband? Because he did it to me first. That's as honest as I can be, and I know the truth is sad. Please put yourself in my shoes. I had been unhappily married for ten years, with a man who was

unfaithful to me constantly. I was emotionally depleted. What was I trying to accomplish? To obtain from that other man all the love, attention, tenderness I had unselfishly given my husband through our marriage. I wanted to know what it felt to be intensively loved by someone. Like I had loved my husband. And ultimately, I had an affair because I wanted to get even. I wanted my husband to feel as jealous, as sad, as angry, and as hurt as I had felt for ten years. I no longer loved myself. I no longer saw my person as a desirable, attractive human being. It was incredible, almost a miracle to find someone else who did.—Linda

Let's get a bit nerdy here. Anthropologists and scientists claim that infidelity makes sense. Monogamy is a romantic idea, not a practical one. After all, we don't see monogamy throughout nature; most animal species have many sexual partners. Blame evolution. Blame the innate desire to spread the seed. Blame it on horniness. Our genetic material is supposed to be put in many baskets. If you want a Wall Street analogy, you don't invest your funds in one single stock.

Science can also describe the distinctions between female and male infidelity. Think about it, most male animals need to perform for just a few minutes, and voila: They've reproduced. Don't forget their amazing capability to do it with many partners. Same species, different species, as long as it has a pulse. Females, on the contrary, are more limited on this matter. They have to be available, and they also seek only healthy specimens to copulate. Once again, the window of opportunity is ample for males and quite limited for females.

Now, let's go back to reality. Not because chimpanzees and lions do it; we have to. We do plenty of stuff differently than animals: We send our kids to school, we vote, we pray, we binge on our favorite TV show, and we mix pineapples and pizza (and think it is an excellent idea). So the social, romantic reasons to not betray our partners are valid. Is it part of our mental evolution?

Other studies show that couples who have kids are more inclined to cheat than those who don't. Now, before your twisted mind starts ranting about a Freud-like factor here, this has nothing to do with kids per se. It has to do with the amount of stress parents endure. And unless you've told a younger version of yourself one hundred times to put on her shoes, or yelled at a door because your teenager slammed it on you, or tried to drink lukewarm coffee just before your six-month-old poops again, then you have no idea.

Tara would never have guessed she would be one of those: a wife who cheated on her husband. It was never her intention, and before she could adequately process it, she was way past the fling. "I didn't wake up and think to myself: here's a thought, I would very much like to have an affair." Nonetheless, it happened.

> This is the truth: People who have flings or affairs are trying to find whatever is lacking in their marriage. And something was fundamentally wrong with mine, but I quite didn't realize it or accept it, until I was already involved with someone else. We started as coworkers who got along pretty well. Then we turned into friends. Then we became friends who flirted. Then we turned into lovers. For me, it was like drinking a whole bottle of wine; at first, you don't realize how drunk are you getting. You are eating dinner, talking with friends, listening to music. You have all of these distractors. And right before saying goodnight, you realize the bottle is empty, and you are hammered.—Tara

Tara excellently described her process. This is the perfect way to explain a woman cheating: it is a process, with steps and stages. Tara did not go to happy hour and kiss the tipsy guy next to her, out of the blue. The nature of her relationship evolved, probably at the same time her marriage got deflated.

Mindy went through something similar:

> People need to understand that on many occasions, infidelity is the last thing on our minds. Everything starts like an innocent, harmless friendship. Then it progresses into something more because you are unhappy with your

husband. For seven years, I was the financial supporter of my house. My husband and two kids relied on me for everything. I was exhausted and angry all the time. We went through every stage: marriage counseling, ultimatums, terrible months filled with anxiety. You cannot think of a single thing I did not try to save my relationship. Then I had an affair. You want to hear the irony? My husband forgave me for it and asked me for another chance. But it was too late. Ten months later, I was asking for a divorce and feeling as free and happy as I never thought I could.

Debunking Myths

1. Women are unfaithful because they want to finish their marriages.

   Can we print this in bold? In general, women look elsewhere because what's in front of them is not satisfying enough. In every aspect. Some women feel neglected emotionally; others complain about the little time their spouse spends with them. Sometimes, the problem resides in the bedroom. Let's hear from Charlize:

   I named my first husband's penis Mr. Roboto. He could go on and on. Ten years of marriage, and Mr. Roboto never failed us. It was paradise in the bedroom, but it was hell everywhere else. He upset me constantly. He was a professional mess. The sex was great, sure, but can you live out of it? After too many fights, my libido went down. We were both so startled we even went to a doctor. I took pills, tried different things. But nothing could bring me pleasure anymore. Until I went to counseling and figured it out. Whatever I was feeling inside, my frustration was reflected in the bedroom.

2. Beginning an affair is a rash impulse.

   We've talked about it. We are pragmatic beings. We design and plan. Who, in their clear mind, would assume that cheating is purely impulsive? It's not a decision females take lightly. And be aware of this: After a woman cheats, she rarely goes back. It takes her months, probably years, to make the decision. But once she crosses the threshold, she will not hit reverse to a life of misery. Ask your dog, and give him a steak for dinner once. The next day, do the same. After a week, try to feed him his nasty old dog food. He won't like it. Dogs appreciate change if it involves improvement; that's a pet, so how about us women?

A famous therapist was intrigued by this inquiry: Why do women cheat? So he sent out an email and asked hundreds of his followers. The responses, although many, fell into three simple categories: "I need more sex," "I am bored/am neglected/feel unloved," or "He cheated, so I want to even the score."

Where is the justification? If you ask men why they cheat, they come up with something like "I fell into temptation" or "I wanted to try something else." Rarely will they speak about their marriage, like it has nothing to do with it. On the other hand, women cheat because they give up after years of trying to change their current situation ("I tried for years; he never listens; he listens but refuses to change; he swears he will change but never does"). Okay, that sounds like a defeat. In reality, it means freedom.

Women are strong individuals. Hard-working, compassionate, and passionate about everything they do. That includes their relationship. They rarely half-commit to something. But this can mean two different things in marriage; if they are happy, they'll do everything in their power to stay that way and continue with the relationship. If they cheat, however, they will not do it casually. If your wife cheats on you, most likely, she has already moved on.

I made the first mistake by marrying the wrong guy. Reality struck harder once we became parents. If I was being ignored before, it was worse afterward. I felt trapped. I was receiving no attention from him whatsoever. For instance, during one Christmas, he went to spend it with his mother without even inviting me. He didn't talk to me rudely; he just didn't speak to me at all! Loving words flew out of the window, as well. And sex periodically lessened over time. It became once a month, and then, once a year. How can you not fall out of love if your husband suddenly becomes your roommate? I took refuge in a wonderful man who gave me the comfort and strength I needed to finish my marriage.—Peggy

When the Spark Has Gone

Magazines and blogs are filled with these words: "Keep the spark alive." It can sound corny, but it is so true. Modern people and modern couples have become so lazy; they think the flame and passion will continue, no matter what. Trust me, the moment your wife no longer asks about your whereabouts and spends quality time with you, she is pleased and happy when you're not home. Oh-oh, the spark has gone. One thing is to trust your partner and confide in them. But a certain level of personal space must be maintained. The other aspect refers to the romantic actions. It's unrealistic to believe you'll be as spirited and passionate as when you're first dating; this requires an intentional effort, folks.

Here are a few symptoms of the spark being long gone in your relationship:

1. Your "goodnight routine" is over. You know, kissing each other and saying, "I love you. Thanks for another great day," or even, "You're the sexiest man to take out the garbage in the whole block." Not a big talker? How about cuddling? Not necessarily leading to sex. One big, warm embrace.
2. You don't have sex. The frequency of it is entirely up to you and your partner. But if you only hit the sack once a year, that's not a great sign.
3. You stop doing things together. Every couple has their own idiosyncrasy. Some play golf together; others like to shop together or do the garden, cook, watch infomercials; you name it. What linked you and your partner in the past is one of the pillars of your relationship. If that support collapses, well, you know what happens to a building that's lost its foundation.

4. You don't date anymore. I know what you're going to say: I got married so I could stop dating. And I'm with you. But do you remember the butterflies in your stomach? How excited were you with each call, each deep conversation? How you spent hours thinking about what to wear? You still need those. Probably not as often as before. But yes, basically, you need to take off your sweats once in a while, put a little mascara, take off the bib smelling like breast milk hanging eternally from your shoulder, and go on a date. The conversation shouldn't revolve around mundane issues like the rent or how Mrs. Simpson called your teenager a snobby mess. You should talk about the moon and the stars, whether there's life on Pluto, how beautiful you look in your green dress (the twins still look good), and such. Sparkle, sparkle, sparkle. You have the rest of the month to visit reality. Just for one night, pretend you are dating.

5. You sleep in different bedrooms. Now, this can start as an innocent step, especially if you have a newborn. But once that stage is over, what's your excuse? He snores too loud? She yells in her sleep? What? Didn't you commit so you could sleep together in the first place?

6. You let yourself go. I get you; trust me. You're exhausted. You've brought human beings through your vagina. That's not easy. You feed them and tend to them. Even if you don't have kids, there's the temptation. Why do I bother putting heels on if these sneakers are as comfortable? My husband likes me au natural, so why wear makeup? That train of thought leads to a dangerous zone. The zone of "Why do I bother washing my hair? It will get dirty again," or "Why should I change my dirty clothes? I want to be responsible with the planet?" Okay, but this may mean you stink worse than a wet sock. Nobody is asking you to look like Miss Universe. But beautiful hair, clean clothes, you know? Cover the basics.

7. You don't pay compliments to each other. Listing your spouse's defects can be an addicting hobby. That's naming all the things he or she sucks at (I have like ten ideas popping in my mind already). Now think about this: When was the last time you paid

a compliment? When was the last time you thanked your spouse for something great he or she did for you? If you can't see the good in your partner, then you are doomed. But you are equally driving towards failure if you do see the greatness and refuse to verbalize it. Your partner needs to hear from your lips how much you admire her or him.

8. You don't celebrate special occasions anymore. When my cousin first got married, she and her husband were going through a rough patch financially. So they made a promise: no gifts or dinners during their birthdays, anniversaries, Christmas, and such. They convinced themselves those celebrations were marketing strategies that made people spend money they didn't have. After their second year of marriage, my cousin found herself washing her socks downstairs while her husband fell asleep at the couch; it was Christmas at midnight. She knew it. It wasn't about the presents or the expensive dinner. It was about maintaining the joy between them. Celebrate together means staying together.

9. You do have sex, but it's not pleasurable. Robotic sex can be as bad as no sex at all. It is not filling a requisite; it is supposed to be enjoyable. Selfish sex, when you're in a race to see who gets satisfied first, is also a terrible sign. That doesn't sound romantic at all.

10. You'd rather spend your free time with friends or family than with your partner. This, too, can sound innocent. You have the afternoon free, and instead of doing something fun with your hubby, you call your best friend. What's wrong with that? Nothing, if it only happens once in a while. But when spending time with other people is the norm, then you have a problem. You don't enjoy each other's company anymore. You've run out of things to talk about. The less time you are together, the better.

There are many other signs you should watch. For instance, our mothers may have complained about our fathers falling asleep in front of the TV instead of talking to them. Modern times have brought a new enemy: social media. Make this comparison: How much time you spend on your smartphone versus how much quality time you have with your partner?

Do you still hold hands? Do you go to bed at the same time? These are foolish, romantic activities. They are symptoms of a healthy relationship. What's the worst sign of all? Cheating. Infidelity is irrefutable proof that the spark has gone.

After six years, there was nothing remotely romantic in our relationship. I wanted to see the world and travel; my husband wanted to stay home all the time. He did not want kids; I did. I constantly wanted to have sex; he preferred to sleep. I am one of those seize-the-day type of person; he was more "I just want to be comfortable." Of course, I was not satisfied with my relationship, but I thought that was marriage. You were doomed. You chose this; no going back. Then one night, my friends took me out to a bar. My husband, of course, didn't want to go. After a couple of drinks, I spotted the most gorgeous man I'd ever seen. He approached me, and we began to talk. I flirted shamelessly, and we danced all night. When it was time to go home, we exchanged phone numbers.

One the way home, something ignited in me. Nothing had indeed happened, but that handsome man was the push I needed. I told my husband I wasn't happy; I asked him to change, to try with me to save our marriage. He agreed to work on our relationship, but he did it reluctantly, as if he thought our marriage was okay as it was. I really tried. I stopped pressing him to go out; I tried silly ideas like movie night at home and proposed things I knew he would like. I put my life dreams aside to try to reconnect to this man I had pledged eternal love to.

To my surprise, my efforts made him even more distant. I went from being bored to feeling lonely and sad all the time. I felt that my presence repulsed him; after a few months, I couldn't take his disdain anymore and asked him for a divorce. Now, I am engaged to a man who fulfills my needs; he loves traveling, he likes challenges, he dreams about having children. And he likes to sleep with me. The feelings of remorse came, of course, but that single night showed me what I wanted. That marriage was not right for me.—Natalie

I was married for twelve years. It was my second marriage. The first one ended because, although the sex was great, the rest was not. On this one, there was admiration and intimacy, but things in the bedroom were less than perfect. For some reason, we could not connect in that way. I am not sure how much time he lied to me, but I lied constantly. Each time we slept together, I said it was great. I faked it. I was afraid to hurt his feelings, until one day, I couldn't take it anymore. We had to do something about it. To my dismay, he took it very well. He agreed we should get professional help; this made me love him and admire him even more. We made an appointment. I was finally getting it all: a great, devoted husband, a hard worker, and now, someone who would make my knees buckle with passion. Guess what? Therapy worked. The sex improved considerably. Was I the luckiest woman alive? Nope. Because as soon as things in the bedroom improved, the rest of my relationship fell apart. I soon started to feel as he performed great in the bedroom to prove me something; to stand his point. He wanted to show me he could be a great lover. I was shocked; there was no intimacy, no communication, no connection. All the things that I had adored from my relationship were gone. When I talked to him, he swore my comments did not hurt him and we were supposed to trust in each other anyways. But my marriage for some reason fell apart. I guess I will never understand it. The moment I went 100 percent sincere, he pushed me away forever.—Trista

Money issues are also a buzzkill:

> My husband pushed me to have an affair. It may sound
> ridiculous, but it is the truth. I never sneaked around or
> lied about who I was seeing. I had this best friend; we've
> been friends for fifteen years. He was the one I turned to
> when I was sad, angry, or in any type of trouble. I never
> wondered if I was attracted to him; maybe I did not want
> to find out. I stayed with my husband because it was the
> responsible thing to do, to stay married. To keep my vows.
> But every time I needed a shoulder to cry or someone to
> celebrate with, my husband told me to call my friend
> instead. So I did. The last string broke when he began to
> expect me to support him financially. I was already taking
> care of the groceries, the kids, our schedules, our house. I
> wasn't receiving anything from him: attention, sex, love.
> And now, not even money! What good was this marriage
> for me? I started to see my friend more often. At first, I
> told myself it was because I needed to vent. But soon, I
> found myself enjoying his company on a different level.
> Just before crossing the line, I spoke to my husband. I
> said, "Either you get the act together, and you turn into
> the husband I need (and the father my kids deserved) or
> we are done." One year later, I found myself sleeping with
> my friend, my marriage over, and uncertainty about my
> future, that doesn't felt that bad.—Jenny

A man cheats on his wife with his secretary, his neighbor, the girl in
the bar. He's never thinking, *Where is this going? Is my marriage over?* If
these thoughts cross his mind, the reason is his lover pushed them into
his brain. For a guy, a lover is an inferior version of his wife. He married
the other lady for a reason. She is the one, the mother of her children, the
one he takes back to his parents, the one he brags about in the office. The
mistress is just another girl he sleeps with. She's probably not the first and
definitely not the last.

But be wary of the woman who cheats. Because the moment she lies down on that bed, she has made a commitment. Not to her lover, not necessarily. But to herself: no, never be treated like she was before. When she's having an affair, she knows things will never be the same. She's moved on. You have lost her.

Women are patient and caring, until they are not. Unfair or not, it is our true nature. So work on the spark, rekindle the feelings that linked you in the first place, because if her heel is out the door, that means her heart is already miles away.

Chapter 7

FAMILY DRAMA

No matter how loving a family is, everyone goes through conflict. While quarreling is usual, expected, and sometimes needed for a relationship, unfortunately, family conflicts tend to escalate faster. Moreover, two family members who hurt each other rarely recover from it. That saying of "Family is family" is a double-edged sword; yes, you try to be more understanding, but heck. You expect better treatment from those who share your blood, genes, and house. But as a wise lady told me, "Sometimes, your closest are the worst." (Ach! Need some band-aids on that one, right?)

Now, conflict is not spontaneous. I mean, a problem does not create itself; someone starts it. So your brother Billy told on you with Mummy, saying, "She started it!" C'mon, we both know he was right; you did say your All-Star Barbie could take his He-Man any day of the week, and that's when the slapping and pinching began. Poor misunderstood Billy; he was correct. Someone always starts it.

You could argue and say that all of this is normal. It's normal to have a noisy aunt who comments on every single one of your Facebook posts (Get a life, Auntie Vivian), it's common to have a jealous sister who still fights to have your parents' attention, it's normal to have a mother-in-law messing with your hubby's brain. "Normal?" you could ask. Yes.

Now, hold your horses and take a deep drag of your Lucky Strike. Nah! I don't miss it at all. Cigarettes: B-a-d. Functional lungs: G-o-o-d. I didn't say the average equals good and desirable. Normal means it's conventional; it is the norm. Men buns and shapeless, humongous t-shirts (or is it sweaters?) are the norm for millennials, but for God's sake, that doesn't mean they are beautiful or great. Agreed?

Among all the mental disorders on the spectrum, there are two singular characters we will discuss: the attention-seeking drama queen (which, excuse me, applies to men as well) and the prolific liar.

Let's begin with the liar.

Lying, my friends, is the art of deception. A lie embeds a cute paradox; you often lie because telling the truth will have a much worse outcome. But if you do get caught, then the punishment is worse than the truth, meaning, you shouldn't have lied. (See what I did there? The *Back to the Future* meets George Orwell and Pinocchio analogy?)

So why do people lie? Because the vast majority of the time, they can get away with it. Not all lies are the same, of course. It's like saying that everyone at Starbucks orders just coffee. I mean, there's a massive difference between a black Americano and a venti half-soy nonfat organic vanilla double-shot gingerbread frappuccino, extra hot with foam, double blended, one Sweet 'n' Low and one Nutrasweet (Thank you, Chester! You are the only barista who gets me).

The same goes with lies. White lies are nonserious, nonthreatening disguised versions of the truth, usually resorted to when that person doesn't want to hurt someone's feelings. Like when your mom told you there was a thousand-word-limit for each person to speak during the day; the poor woman did it so you could stop your babbling. She couldn't even listen to her thoughts anymore. Or when at a Christmas party, your cousin asks what you think of her new boyfriend, and you say, "He seems great," although he is self-centered and spoke all night about how his mommy picked up the sweater he's wearing (which says "Jingle My Bells"), and by the way, you caught him checking out your cleavage while you leaned over.

Those lies are understandable to a certain point; it's not your place to go all blunt with everyone all the time. We have filters to discern what to say and what to keep to ourselves. False statements are also used by people to save themselves from trouble or embarrassment. "No, I don't have any questions," you say at the end of the PTA meeting. But you were daydreaming about the bid you did earlier for that gorgeous teapot and did not pay attention to Miss Atkinson. "I am actually working on it" is everyone's favorite excuse at work when you are asked about your progress on a project, and surely, you are working on everything except that.

No matter the size of the lie or the reason behind it, lying to a family member is bound to create conflict. Lies also come in different forms; for example, let's say that one person lies about knowing how to speak the hundreds of dialects from India, and another person claims to be the reincarnation of Saint Francis of Assisi, who also has a message from heaven. Sadly, for the second person, that particular lie can cause much more distress to people than the first.

Embellishing the Truth

Don't that sound beautiful? It's like saying, "Forgive me, I just excreted an invisible gaseous substance via my vocal cavity," instead of merely saying, "Sorry, mate. I just belched." (Those flaming hot Cheetos were worth it.)

The embellishment of the truth is mostly an exaggeration, a phrase that carries a dash of realness and some made-up portion. These are super common during job interviews and first dates and any situation where you want to make a great impression. In fact, it has been said that most people lie about the number of sexual partners they've had. You know, two sounds like a loser, but two hundred sounds like you should go into the Guinness records, along with Mick Jagger. (Seriously, Mick? Four thousand?)

When someone in the family embellishes the truth or exaggerates what happened to them, it can be hilarious ("My darling Brenda was actually nominated for a Nobel Prize, but she couldn't accept it because it interfered with her Hollywood career.") or frustrating; it rarely causes family conflict.

Why do people do it? People tend to disguise aspects of their lives they are dissatisfied with. You may have a friend who's always bragging about how perfect her relationship is. Her husband is a gentleman, and being married feels like sleeping on a bed of roses with strawberries and champagne. But you know that she fights with her spouse all the time, and they've almost called it quits many times.

Same happens with family members. Parents tend to exaggerate their children's achievements and traits, especially when they feel competitive around other siblings. "Really? Was Scott accepted at Yale? Well, so was Pete did too, along with Harvard and Oxford. But he decided to stay home and begin his career in management." What's a mother going to say? "Oh, really? Well, my boy couldn't even get accepted in community college, so he got a part-time job at McDonald's while he figures it out."

So what's the recommendation here? Patience. I know you want to confront them or, at least, roll your eyes. But as long as these exaggerations don't interfere with anyone or cause any harm, there's not much to do here. Shrug your way out of them. Because believe me, when it comes to lies, there's a lot worse you can suffer. Worse than your brother exaggerating about his wife's fantastic cooking skills? Oh, dear. Much worse.

Compulsive Liars

These people have for sure entered the big leagues. People who are compulsive liars lie as a habit. They also display some textbook behavior: they sweat, avoid eye contact, stutter, and ramble, and after confronted, they start to say more lies to cover the initial lies. They are not a treat to be around, but they are super easy to spot.

This is Liam's encounter with a girl who was a compulsive liar:

> I was quite introverted when I first entered high school. Then I met Sasha. She was so cool; I could not believe someone like that had an interest in hanging out with me. She was a model, was friends with a famous local celebrity, and was an Olympic-level runner. Smart, fashionable, and beautiful. Although she was three years older than me, I was somehow astonished she spent time with a geeky freshman, but I enjoyed it nonetheless.

> One time, she offered me a ride in her new Corvette; she got it as a birthday present from her parents. I sort of got the feeling she thought I was going to say no, but I accepted. When we were walking through the parking lot, she approached an old Honda Civic. She went white and exclaimed, "Shit, I forgot to tell you; the car is still in

the agency, and they gave me this piece of junk just for a couple of days."

So that made me suspicious. I decided to check some things to put her on the spot. Like when I asked her the name of her modeling agency because my friend was interested. Sasha began to stutter and finally blurted out that they were very private and exclusive. As soon as I got home, I started googling some of the stuff she had said to me. Turned out the celebrity she was supposed to be friends with had died ten years ago. Also, the time she said was her personal record on the fifteen hundred meters was like one minute less than the world record.

I couldn't help myself and confronted her about this last one. She angrily said, "Dumbass, records are meant to be broken." And she never spoke to me again. Not that I wanted to be friends with a compulsive liar anyway.

Pathological Liars

Pathological liars, like compulsive ones, lie indiscriminately, but it comes effortlessly. In fact, lying is so natural to them that telling the truth is awkward, uncomfortable, and uncommon. It's like me with the gym. My natural approach is to sit snuggly on my sofa, with the AC on (Thank you, global warming), watching Netflix and getting up just to get a refill. The unnatural, troublesome way to go is to get up at 5 a.m. for a daily run, followed by a power green juice. It just isn't me. Well, that's how pathological liars behave. They are not wired that way.

They are also experts in their field; they are not so easy to spot, and they have become so fantastically skilled at telling falsehoods that they start to believe them. To understand a little bit more about pathological liars, and detect if your family member is one, here are some facts about them:

Pathological lying is usually connected to a mental illness, such as multiple personality disorder.

My aunt [Mother's youngest sister] is a compulsive liar, and it has got to the point where I feel I should cut her out of our lives. Although when she was young, she was beautiful (still is), popular, and successful, she has been struggling with mental issues that go far back. She was diagnosed with narcissistic syndrome and other issues but refuses to follow therapy or go to counseling. The conflicts she has created in our family are endless, especially when it comes to situations that can benefit her directly. Now that she is romantically involved with someone, things have gotten worse. They both destroyed our family and made up false accusations, especially about my sister and I, since we are the ones who won't tolerate her behavior. My parents refuse to reprimand her as they are afraid she may harm herself, which I see as a too remote of a possibility, and this has caused some friction between them. Although I appreciate how hard it is to live with a mental illness, I don't believe that this fully excuses her actions.

The number one goal of pathological liars is to make themselves look better; therefore, it makes sense that narcissists are also liars.

Pathological liars have different hormone levels than most people.

Please don't tell me that aside from my indigestion, anxiety, and the occasional hot flash (I swear it feels like Ethiopia on steroids inside), hormones are also to blame for lying habits?

Well, scientists believe it. And those guys spent their best years combining viscous, gooey substances in the lab instead of attending the Kappa-Lambda spring week, so I personally trust them.

Liars have the opposite ratio of cortisol and testosterone than most of us; therefore, hormone levels do play a role in their lying.

They tend to lie about medical issues.

I have a friend who lies about her health all the time. She's one of those people who hears about a disease and immediately thinks she has it. A few years ago, she left her friends befuddled when she sadly announced she had distemper, which only attacks animals. I had never considered her a pathological liar; I have only thought of her as my go-to person if I require a weird pill or medicine, 'cause she's got them all. Now that I think about it, she has a severe mental disturbance. One time, she even had an endoscopy, for no reason at all. Well, she did say they offered a discount at the hospital, and lately, she felt her esophagus was just not right.

Most pathological liars believe their own lies.

When I got engaged, my boyfriend got me an awful ring. Since I have always been an outspoken person, after the celebration, I casually mentioned that I wanted to change it. This thing was supposed to be on my finger for eternity. Might as well get something I actually liked. Since the ring came in a famous store's little box, I suggested to my boyfriend that we go there the next day, but after some stuttering, he admitted the ring was actually from his mother. She had given the hideous ring to my boyfriend so he wouldn't spend his money on me. With the promise of a new ring ahead, the next day, the entire family went to have dinner. I noticed my boyfriend's brother's wife looking at my ring and giggling.

I said, "Is everything okay?"

She maliciously replied, "I'm sorry. I probably shouldn't say this, but when Jeff [her husband] proposed, he gave me the ring you are wearing. I thought it was awful, so he went to New York and got my ring at Tiffany's. Sorry."

I turned to her and asked, "Can you show me your ring? See? It looks very similar to mine."

She stopped smiling immediately and said, "I don't think so."

"Yes, look at how the flowers blend with the tiny rock. These rings come from the exact same place."

Now I was giggling, while she was astonished and swallowing the venom. Before that, my boyfriend had told me that when she returned the ring, my mother-in-law had given Jeff another one of her ugly rings. That ring did not come from New York; it came from my MIL's jewelry chest!

Since she would never admit it, she keeps telling people about how her beloved husband traveled all the way to the Big Apple to get her the perfect ring, when in fact, it had been next to my MIL's cotton knickers for over twenty years. I now realize that she is such a liar, she genuinely believes all the crazy statements that come out of her mouth.

When prolific liars had traumatic events or a stressful childhood, they often start to believe their false statements. They become so detached from reality, almost delusional, that they cannot tell the difference anymore.

Many times, a pathological liar is trying to avoid shame. Remorse does not play a role here; only a professional is capable of actually changing them.

It's difficult to treat adult liars.

We have all lied at one point in our lives, especially during childhood. Kids lie all the time, to avoid trouble, to get what they want, and to relieve anxiety. To be fair, we lie to our kids all the time as well; between Santa, the Tooth Fairy, the Easter Bunny, Mickey, and "Daddy and I were just dancing in bed." You can't really blame them for following our steps. With a bit of patience and common sense, we can correct this nasty habit when they are young.

Adult liars are much harder to correct. We are talking about decades of chronic and automatic lying. Clinical therapists say it is not impossible to treat them, presuming they actually want to go to therapy, but it's challenging, nonetheless.

Pathological liars lie to relieve anxiety.

Sometimes, the lying starts as a defense mechanism after a traumatic event. A person can be perfectly average, then something severe happens, and Bam. Falseland begins.

A year ago, my eldest sister got divorced. From that point on, she has become unpredictable and lies all the time. She even lies about silly stuff such as what she's doing that day.

The worse part of it is how she manipulates and hurts her teenage son by making up stories about her ex-husband. She tells him his daddy doesn't care about him; she does not care how her ex-husband tries so hard to be a part of their son's life. She has gotten to the point of making up weird stories about our own father. It all points out to portraying men as evil creatures. She is obsessed and delusional. I get that she went under a lot of stress with her divorce, yet I do not understand how she thinks lying will help her move on.

Lying can be addictive.

Have you ever gone to a casino? Have you seen the people playing slot machines? The objective is to eventually hit the jackpot. Nonetheless, the chances are quite slim. Why do people keep doing it, then? Because of two reasons: One, the action of pulling the lever becomes automatic; it's like an instinctive action: the lever goes down, the lever goes up. Second, because you never know when you will win, and that level of anticipation, fear, and anxiety is absolutely addictive. (Okay, I lied; there's a third reason: a delicious ice-cold Bahama Mama with a little umbrella on top. Yeah! You keep them coming, honey!)

The same happens with a pathological liar. Liars don't know when or if they will get caught. And this unnerving emotion keeps them going.

Do you live with a pathological liar?

It may be hard for you to know whether you have a compulsive or pathological liar in your family; some of them are quite good at hiding their true self. Here are a few questions that can help you spot them:

- Does that person always lie about small, unimportant things? When people lie continually, even about silly things such as what they had for dinner last night, most likely, they also lie about important things.
- If caught, does that person begin to fabricate an intricate story to justify the lie they told in the first place? Pathological liars will

rarely accept the truth; instead, they proceed to come up with the most imaginative ways to cover up their lies.

- Do they become aggressive when challenged about a statement? Pathological liars will jump in one second, from being calmed and relax to get all Hulk-level when you ask for proof about what they are saying.
- Have you ever caught that person contradicting themselves? Like when your cousin Lara told everyone she was in the Peace Corps in 1999, but then you ask, "But I thought you said you were in college in 1999," and then she says, "Oh, I studied my major in the Peace Corps." But then you keep going: "But I thought you said you had earned your major at NASA?" and Lara starts fuming, grows all red, and snaps, "I was in the Peace Corps in space, okay?" and you proceed to shut up.
- Does your family member show remorse about lying? Pathological liars rarely feel they are doing something wrong by telling false statements; in fact, they believe them. So they are more concerned about being perceived as untrustworthy than about the damage they can cause.

How do you deal with a pathological liar in your life?

The best approach is to avoid confronting them aggressively. The key is to firmly, but politely, confront them with the truth. It helps a great deal if you have tangible evidence. Living with a pathological liar is a burden; loving one is overwhelming. If things get out of hand or the lying is escalating, the best thing is to get professional help.

Histrionic Personality Disorder (aka Drama Queen)

Kurt texted me at 8 p.m., sobbing and wailing. The drama began early in the morning; it was his hair. After thirty minutes of close examination, he convinced himself he was going bald. He then left for work, and albeit he has a great job and does fairly well, he was sure his boss had given him a nasty look over the vending machine, which made him sick and ran to the bathroom. Seeking for some comforting words, he called his romantic partner, who tried his best to console him; however, Kurt perceived him as distant and aloof and thought he wanted to break up with him. So he locked himself in the bathroom to cry for over one hour, missed an important meeting, and prevented anyone else from using the toilet. Kurt is a drama queen.

He reacts to ordinary occurrences with excessive emotion and behaves as he were performing on a Broadway stage. He is the type of friend who will consume three hours of your precious time to complain about his miserable life; in other words, that he received the socks he ordered from Amazon in blush pink when he specifically asked for coral, while you try your best not to slap him with your quesadilla. Drama queens love you one minute, only to hate you the next because you didn't react how they wanted.

Histrionic personality disorder can be spotted when someone always seeks attention, overreacts at the smallest provocation, and yet displays seductive behavior, a "can't live with them; can't live without them" sort of situation. People suffering this syndrome overdramatize situations, and of course, this ends up hurting relationships.

Drama queens are uncomfortable when they are not the center of attention. They can embarrass their families by acting socially inappropriate, such as embracing someone they barely know or having a public tantrum. It doesn't matter where they are: at work, at a family reunion, at the Morbid Anatomy Museum (impressed me to the bones, no pun intended); they absolutely have to be the center of attention, and they talk about themselves nonstop.

Is your family member a drama queen?

Hmm, let's see:

- Is she self-centered to the point of getting upset when someone else is the focus of attention?
- Does she always seek approval?

- Does she use her looks to allure people?
- Does she rapidly switch her emotional state, like a roller coaster?
- Is she overly dramatic?
- Does she display lots of emotion over minor setbacks?

These are the definitive symptoms of a drama queen:

If someone says, "I don't like drama" or "I don't do drama," they do. At some point in our lives, we all overreact; it's natural.

No accountability for behavior. So most of the problem is created by their overreaction. However, they rarely see themselves as part of the problem. In fact, they always find someone else to blame. And when they do take on the blame, it's to portray the role of a victim and seek attention by acting dramatically.

Trolling with capital T. Drama lures more drama. Attention-seekers need to have more drama to carry on. If no one follows along, they've got nothing else going for them. So they seek out others to play along with their toxic behavior. They also love to talk behind people's backs and gossip. Drama queens retain valuable information and use it for their benefit, destroying relationships. Dana was friends with my friend's sister-in-law. One time, my friend was complaining about her in-laws and suddenly turned to Dana and said, "I know you're really close to my sister-in-law, please don't say anything. I don't want to create a problem. I am just venting."

Dana laughed and said, "My lips are sealed. And I see your point; your sister-in-law can be quite a bitch, and between you and me, I have no idea how her husband stands close to her. She has the most fetid breath I've ever smelled. Seems like something died in her mouth."

We all sort of laughed but thought she was kind of harsh. You know, it's one thing to call your sister-in-law a bitch but another one to discuss her personal hygiene. Anyway, as we expected, at the precise moment when she needed it, Dana told that poor foul-smelling girl that my friend had said those nasty things about her. The family was outraged, and a significant conflict developed. My poor friend spent months sucking up to her sister-in-law, while Dana was fresh as a daisy.

Relationships are a matter of winning or losing. If you are married to a drama queen or are related to one, you may have realized every single interaction is potentially adversarial for them. They turn every conversation into a competition that they must win, of course.

Justification is their modus operandi. Drama-seekers find being justified more critical than being effective. They'd rather win a dull, meaningless battle while losing the war. In other terms, they prefer creating conflict that makes them look good than preserving a relationship. Conflict is their weapon; gossiping and scheming is their ammunition. They use all their energy to complicate an issue, instead of resolving it. The aftermath? Impaired relationships, toxic environments, wasted time, and resources.

This is Romy's story:

> We never knew how much of a drama queen my middle sister Sandra was until my wedding day. Since she is older than me, she was sort of upset that I got married first, and she began to show some crazy behavior in preparation for my big day. For instance, during my bachelorette party, she grabbed my spot from the beginning, took over the karaoke microphone for most of the night, and had the photographer take pictures of her with my guests, without me. But the worst happened during the actual wedding.
>
> We were about to take the family picture when her boyfriend's son fell asleep (he was previously married). After an hour complaining about how the wind was messing her hair and how the grass was making her sneeze, she started the biggest of tantrums because she didn't want the kid (not even two years old) to be in the picture with his eyes closed. I said it was fine, but she wouldn't have it and demanded her boyfriend wake up her son. Her poor boyfriend, not wanting to ruin our moment, politely said he was not going to be in the picture and carried his boy to the back of the room. Attempting to lessen the scandal, I said it was fine and told the photographer to carry on.
>
> My sister then began wailing and sobbing uncontrollably, telling my parents how insensitive I was to ask her boyfriend

to not be in the family picture. She cried so hard her makeup got ruined, and they had to fix her, which took around twenty minutes. During that time, my entire family tried to console her, while I hyperventilated in a corner. What was supposed to be a fun, memorable moment turned into a nightmare, thanks to her dramatic behavior.

Why, God, why?

What causes this problematic behavior? No one knows for sure. Some experts say it all tracks down to our childhood (doesn't it all?); others claim our genes may be involved. And while you may think that it is more common in women than men, the truth is, we don't know for sure.

How do you stop the madness, then?

You guessed it: therapy, therapy, therapy. Confronting them is as effective as the wine and boiled eggs diet. I mean, who wouldn't fall for a meal made up of yummy cholesterol and alcohol? Both of these approaches are well-intentioned but do not work at all. (By the way, the baby food diet is also a ridiculous hoax; leave the Gerber aisle alone, unless you actually have children.)

If working with a drama queen is hard, living with or being related to one can be extremely draining, disturbing, and frustrating. It's like waking up to a bomb of complaints, accusations, and misinterpretations of reality in a high-pitched voice when you haven't even gone to the bathroom yet.

If your family member agrees to go to therapy, you may have to come with them for some sessions. They will exaggerate their symptoms or tell a distorted version of the events. Also, be aware that some drama queens can turn violent and physically hurt themselves or others. Psychologists attribute this to the depression or anxiety linked to this syndrome.

Conclusion

Relationships are hard, especially when we talk about family members. One never knows when to push more or step back. Ultimately, it is a bond you don't want to break up, but at the same time, you wish to maintain some sanity. Trying to fix a family conflict is as uncertain as knowing how long to wait before an avocado is ripe. I mean, one day, it's hard as a rock, and the next day, the damn thing is as spoiled as your cousin Kelly. (Yes, Kelly! Poor Auntie Glendy had to remove the seeds out of your tomatoes.)

It's natural for you to try to take matters in your hands. Confront the liars in your life and cut the drama thread, but that's seldom the solution. In case of an emergency, do not hesitate to call the experts. Meanwhile, know you are not alone. This too shall pass

Summary

It's normal in life to go through phases, for instance personally I was dick whipped, big time mommy's girl and then I got bitchy and became a bit of a narc in my other relationships. It's a learning curve but frankly speaking anyone who gets stuck in a phase like being a full time narc, liar, cheater, daddy pleaser etc is not the norm. All I am saying it does not take an expert to realise something is off when you are on the receiving or giving end. All of the chapters written in my book is just a snippet of our life hurdles. Each chapter is a book on its own. There are plenty of books on diagnosis and medical terminology. However this book is just an eye opener from a common man's point of view expression. Also known as a reasonable man test as used in UK legal field.

In our case would her boyfriend be considered a cheater if he has cheated only 6 times in their 3 year relationship?

What would you a reasonable man say?

Once you are aware of your situation there are plenty of avenues for support be it medical, professional or holistic. The choice is yours. Life is too short for bullshit. We all need to live peacefully and move on to our next elevated level.

Life is too short for bullshit. We all need to live and next!

9 781665 580106